★ HISPANIC STAR

SYLVIA RIVERA

CLAUDIA ROMO EDELMAN
AND **J. GIA LOVING**

ILLUSTRATED BY **CHEYNE GALLARDE**

ROARING BROOK PRESS

NEW YORK

For my mom, who lost her battle to Covid, but whose values live in me every day. I am who I am because she was the best of role models.

For my husband, Richard, and children, Joshua and Tamara, who surround me with their love, their belief in me, and support. They make it all possible.

Most of all, this series is dedicated to the children of tomorrow. We know that you have to see it to be it. We hope these Latino heroes teach you to spread your wings and fly.
—*C. R. E.*

In honor of my movement sister and mother, Sylvia Lee Rivera. Thank you for taking me up on this conversation through the stars. Thank you to each and every queer being before me who lived their fabulous lives in their own way, no matter the decade.

For Tiger, mi amor.

And each of you . . . wild, beautiful young people, growing up in this wild, beautiful world. Make sure to color yourselves into the history books.
—*J. G. L.*

Published by Roaring Brook Press
Roaring Brook Press is a division of Holtzbrinck Publishing Holdings Limited Partnership
120 Broadway, New York, NY 10271 • mackids.com

Copyright © 2023 by We Are All Human Foundation. All rights reserved.
Written by Claudia Romo Edelman and J. Gia Loving.
Illustrated by Cheyne Gallarde.

Our books may be purchased in bulk for promotional, educational, or business use. Please contact your local bookseller or the Macmillan Corporate and Premium Sales Department at (800) 221–7945 ext. 5442 or by email at MacmillanSpecialMarkets@macmillan.com.

Library of Congress Control Number: 2022916426

First edition, 2023
Book design by Julia Bianchi
Printed in the United States of America by Lakeside Book Company, Crawfordsville, Indiana

ISBN 978-1-250-82814-9 (paperback)
10 9 8 7 6 5 4 3 2 1

ISBN 978-1-250-82816-3 (hardcover)
10 9 8 7 6 5 4 3 2 1

A NOTE ON NAMES

The names that we call ourselves play an important role in our identity as individuals. Across different cultures and communities, names are given and chosen at various parts of one's life. Someone may receive their name at birth or after a special ceremony. For some people, choosing their own name can honor a specific change they experience; this can include transgender people who transition across genders or spiritual people who join a community.

For some people, the names they no longer use can bring up negative feelings. One way to show respect for others is by using the name they have most recently chosen to go by.

Note on Sylvia's name: Throughout this book, I refer to Sylvia with the name she chose rather than the one given to her at birth. Sylvia went by both names at various points in her life.

NOTE ON COMMUNITY IDENTITIES: Like our individual names, the labels we use to refer to our community are also important and ever-changing. Throughout this book I refer to people with marginalized gender identities and orientations as transgender and queer people.

—J. G. L.

NOTE ON LANGUAGE: Writing a biography about a person who has transitioned or who identifies as different from the sex assigned at birth requires that we make some choices. For both *Hispanic Star: Sylvia Rivera* and its Spanish companion, we decided to honor Sylvia's identity as a woman from birth. During Sylvia's lifetime, the English pronouns *they/them* were not yet used by transgender/queer persons. In Spanish, similar pronouns were not used then either, and they are yet to be settled in common usage today. Because of this, and to honor Sylvia's identity, we refer to her with feminine pronouns. When we speak of a collective, we use the pronoun *los*, which is consistent with current Spanish usage.

CHAPTER ONE

SHE'S A GIRL

By the midpoint of the twentieth century, the United States had already experienced the booms and busts of its growing global power.

The Great Depression during the 1930s sent the world into an economic crisis and left people in a cloud of uncertainty. While families scraped by to survive, political leaders in Europe were focused on the Second World War, which had begun after the German invasion of Poland in 1939. The United States entered the war following the Japanese bombing of the American naval station, Pearl Harbor, on the Hawaiian island of Oahu in 1941. The demand for wartime soldiers and materials created jobs for Americans and profit for the economy. Not only did World War II pull the United States out of economic depression, it encouraged Americans to believe their financial security was determined by the country's ability to conquer outside enemies.

By the mid-1940s, the United States and Allied nations, such as Great Britain, declared victory in the World War. Shortly after, the United Nations was established with fifty-one nations committing to maintaining peace, while the Allied nations established themselves as permanent members of the newly created UN Security Council. But global tensions soon reemerged as the United States and Soviet Union became superpower rivals in a standoff known as the Cold War that lasted throughout most of the second half of the century.

Within the United States, divisions among Americans also deepened. Many groups of marginalized people banded together to demand change and equality. Women campaigned early in the century for their right to vote. After World War II, they demanded to be included in political discussions that previously only men were welcomed into. Black people and other people of color also spent decades in local communities organizing toward racial justice and the dream of equality for all.

Sylvia Lee Rivera was born into a family that deeply understood the impacts of a divided world. Throughout the first few years of her life, learning how to *make do* with little would need to become second nature.

Sylvia was born on July 2, 1951, at 2:30 a.m. in New York City. Her mother, twenty-two-year-old Carmen Mendoza, birthed Sylvia in the back of a taxicab outside the old Lincoln Hospital in the Bronx. Born with her feet first, Sylvia's grandmother would tease and joke that she had been "born ready to hit the streets." As Sylvia grew older, she laughed about her grandmother's omen but never denied it.

Living in the US with familial roots in Latin America meant the Rivera and Mendoza families had to build their livelihoods from very little. Like other migrant families, they had to adapt to life in the states. Often, newly arrived

migrants could not rely on American state protection or support without also risking further family separation. Nevertheless, they persisted.

Sylvia's parents were young and needed to learn how to sustain a family. Jose Rivera, Sylvia's father, came from a Puerto Rican family. Her mother, Carmen, was raised by a Venezuelan migrant single mother, whom the neighborhood referred to as Viejita.

Shortly after Sylvia was born, Jose left Carmen and their newborn child, Sylvia. Jose returned to reconnect with his daughter when she was four years old. But by then, Sylvia refused to accept Jose as her father.

"I don't have a father!" Sylvia yelled before running out of the apartment.

Carmen entered a new relationship after Jose left the family and gave birth to Sylvia's sibling, her half sister Sonia.

Living with Sonia's father was not easy for Sylvia or her sister. He showed no interest in the children and refused to support Carmen in raising either Sonia or Sylvia. He also struggled to control his anger when upset, and his actions left everyone afraid. Scared for herself and her children, Carmen was desperate to find a way out of his influence. In this desperation, Carmen tragically passed away at a local hospital after poisoning herself.

Although Viejita was devastated by the death of her daughter, Sylvia and Sonia were moved into their grandmother's care. Viejita had spent months trying to support Carmen as she tried to leave her unhealthy relationship. While grieving for her daughter, Viejita found comfort in how Sonia's features resembled young Carmen's. On top of Sonia looking like her mother, she was lighter-skinned than Sylvia was, which was one of the many reasons Viejita treated her grandchildren differently.

Sonia's father eventually returned to remove Sonia from Viejita's care. He set up for Sonia to be adopted by a Puerto Rican couple, as opposed to the Venezuelan-led household of Viejita. Viejita was even more devastated to have lost yet another part of Carmen.

Sadly, Sylvia was left to receive the brunt end of Viejita's despair.

Viejita struggled to care for Sylvia. She was still working through the loss of her daughter, but she had also began to fear who Sylvia may become. From Viejita's perspective, her grandson was trying to become una niña, a girl.

After Sylvia was born, her doctor assumed that she was a boy based on what her body looked like. They then filled in Sylvia's birth certificate gender marker as male. Using what she had learned from watching other women raise children in her family, Carmen began raising Sylvia as a son and gave her a name thought to be fit for a boy.

As Sylvia grew, her family tried to teach her what was expected of boys, like how to act, dress, and even what to dream about. Both Puerto Rican and Venezuelan cultures have clear ideas of what gender should look like and how people should act. Gender has often been used as a way to categorize and control different groups of people. In Latin American cultures, the concept of "machismo," or male dominance, is rewarded, while girls are taught to play a supporting role.

But acting in the ways expected of boys did not come naturally for Sylvia. From early childhood, Sylvia refused to be boxed into the gender roles traditionally held for boys. In the short time she had with her mom, Sylvia learned there were more options for her as her mother relaxed her enforcement of Sylvia's gender.

"Before my mother passed away," Sylvia remembered, "my mother used to dress me in girls' clothes." Over the few years that Carmen had raised Sylvia, she lessened the rigid rules of how Sylvia could explore gender. She let Sylvia play around with her accessories and dress in her clothes. When Sylvia looked interested, Carmen let her try on her heels and makeup.

Viejita usually looked the other way when Carmen let

Sylvia dress in feminine clothes. After Carmen's passing, Viejita eventually bought Sylvia clothes from the girls' section herself.

"My grandmother kept on buying little blouses and girls' slacks until I was about six or seven years old, before I went to school."

Yet as Sylvia reached school age, Viejita's worries about her grandchild's gender expression grew. This created tension between Viejita and Sylvia.

"My grandmother used to come home and find me all dressed up. Just like . . . I'd get [myself] whipped," Sylvia remembered. "'Well, we don't do this. You're one of the boys. I want you to be a mechanic,'" she recalled Viejita telling her.

"I said, 'No, but I want to be a hairdresser. I want to do this. And I want to wear these clothes,'" Sylvia explained.

Outside their home, members of the community disapproved of Sylvia's appearance and gender-bending. They expressed shame and discomfort with how happily feminine Sylvia was. Taking what they understood of their Catholic faith, the community believed anybody who was breaking out of traditionally accepted gender roles was also defying faith. Young Sylvia didn't care much about that, but her grandmother was conflicted.

Viejita's insecurities about raising Sylvia led Viejita to distance herself and try to avoid her responsibility of caring for her grandchild.

At the time Sylvia started school, Viejita became ill and enrolled Sylvia in St. Agnes, a Catholic boarding school. Although Viejita recovered six months later, she delayed bringing Sylvia back home. When Sylvia visited from school on the weekends, Viejita often arranged a different place for Sylvia to stay. Viejita sent Sylvia to live with family friends and sometimes migrant women she sponsored.

With little encouragement to explore her identity, Sylvia tried to understand what about her made the people surrounding her so upset. *Why were the adults in her life not supportive?* Sylvia continued to dream about a world where young people could be free to just be themselves.

Luckily for Sylvia, there were some adults who took their time to show her how special she was. One of these supporters was an upstairs neighbor named Sarah. Sarah was an older woman who had taken notice of the young, sweet girl. The little interactions between Sylvia and Sarah usually included Sylvia complimenting her outfit and accessories, something Sylvia had an eye for. Since Sarah could tell how fascinated she was with pretty jewelry, she often gifted her small trinkets that Viejita couldn't or wouldn't buy. Supportive adults like Sarah helped Sylvia to not only keep moving toward her potential but also to know that it was possible to find people who loved her for who she was.

Fashion helped Sylvia express herself and feel joy. Sylvia was full of creative ideas and dreamed about becoming a hairdresser. In a salon, she could someday transform her clients into the fabulous beings she knew they were. She was excited to use her talents to help those around her realize their beauty!

Sylvia looked forward to school as the place where she felt support as she focused on her goals. She also saw her time at school as time away from her grandmother, where she was safe to be herself. Sylvia made friends with other girls and explored wearing makeup to class. In the same ways adults in the community teased her, kids at school also bullied Sylvia and some staff even treated her as an outcast. *And* in the same way that Sylvia didn't care what adults in the community said about her, she made it clear to her bullies that she wouldn't back down. Over the years, Sylvia's strong heart and bold mouth, as well as her time in school athletics, helped her to develop a reputation of the girl you shouldn't mess with.

While Sylvia tried to avoid conflict and stay safe at school, by the end of elementary school she was forced to decide between her education and her safety.

One day, in the sixth grade, Sylvia found herself in a confrontation with another student. The other student had been bullying her and pressured Sylvia to react. When Sylvia defended herself to avoid being hurt, both she and the other student were sent to the principal's office. Sylvia explained to the school principal that she had been defending herself and was not causing harm— she was actually trying to *avoid* being harmed. Both students were suspended from campus. This didn't make sense for Sylvia. *Why was she in trouble for trying to defend herself?*

After years of being targeted by others and being punished for choosing to care for herself, Sylvia felt desperate and lonely. She wondered if this was a little of what her mother felt before choosing to leave. Sylvia felt that she could not return to a place where she wasn't protected or allowed to protect herself.

WHAT IS TRANSPHOBIA?

TRANSPHOBIA describes the different forms of hate and violence targeted at transgender people. A transgender (or trans) person is someone whose gender is different from the gender they were assigned at birth. In many Western cultures, children are usually split into girls and boys and expected to follow the strict ideas of gender roles. Trans people experience gender differently and sometimes TRANSITION toward a gender that feels right for them.

When people are taught strict rules about gender their entire lives, it can be hard to understand why others would choose to not live out these rules. When they allow curiosity to turn into fear or anger, they may choose to act out these negative feelings onto others; this is transphobia.

Transphobia works to make people feel "othered" and inferior.

Looking at human history around the world, gender and gender expression are much more diverse than a two-option binary. Gender has been experienced differently for humans and celebrated in cultures in a variety of ways throughout history.

Today, transphobia looks like some of the following moments:

- Not believing trans people's experiences or narratives.
- Refusing to use the name or pronouns someone chooses to go by.
- Bringing or encouraging harm to trans people physically.
- Communities kicking someone out because they are trans.

Transphobia hurts everyone. By pressuring trans people to conform to the gender binary, all people are pushed further away from self-determination. The more limiting our options of living life are, the more we limit our own potential. BODILY AUTONOMY, the idea that people have the right to decide what to do with their bodies, is at the center of this issue.

Gender should be fun, free, and enjoyable.

By the time she turned ten, Sylvia boldly refused to hide her truth: She was not a boy, even after so many people tried to convince her otherwise. She was not a boy, even if this meant her community would push her away. She was not a boy, even though the world was determined to force the idea that she was one on her.

She was a young girl whose dreams of the future were growing too big for the box she was born into.

This left a heavy impact on Sylvia.

Just before Sylvia's eleventh birthday, Viejita came home in tears after hearing someone insult Sylvia with a transphobic slur. Although it took time for Viejita to accept that Sylvia was not going through a phase, Viejita had slowly opened her heart back up to her granddaughter. While she had moments of uncertainty, Viejita cared for her family. Hearing her neighbors speak ill of her grandchild was devastating.

"It hurt her so bad because they were doing this to me. And she knew where I was coming from," Sylvia remembered. "She knew."

When community members called attention to Sylvia with mean words, all that was on Sylvia's mind was how embarrassed and hurt Viejita probably was. Viejita felt conflicted between her desire to care for her grandchild and the pressure of her community's expectations. A fear of judgment and cultural rejection led Viejita to hold on to the hope that Sylvia would one day blend in, and she tried to limit the ways she expressed herself. Sylvia felt sympathetic to her grandmother's concerns.

"I had that much respect for my grandmother. I didn't want her to suffer. It wasn't my suffering. I was worrying about her suffering," Sylvia recalled.

Sylvia did not have a safe place to call home with Viejita's support wavering. And she did not have a safe place at school, where she was punished alongside her bullies. When she realized that the adults in her life would not be able to support the person she was becoming, Sylvia decided it would be safer to leave. She needed to find people who would love and care for her, no matter what her gender was.

At only ten years old, Sylvia left her grandmother's home in South Bronx. She took the train to Manhattan, heading south, toward Forty-Second Street, a place she had overheard her family talking about. Apparently, people—girls like her—would sometimes set up camp there when they were kicked out of their family's homes.

She prayed she had heard correctly and went searching for her people.

CHAPTER TWO

FORTY-SECOND STREET

Sylvia left her home and school determined to find people who would accept her for who she was becoming.

Growing up, her family would mention Forty-Second Street as one part of New York City where there were always groups of queer and homeless people living on the street. This usually happened when her family traveled across town on the subway. Seated somewhere in the train would be a group of fabulous-looking women with dramatic expressions and a bold presence. While the strange women mingled with one another and occasionally made a scene, the adults in Sylvia's family passed judgment under their breath.

Sylvia remembered the criticism in her family's voices, but also held on to the memory of seeing these other girls who seemed so free and true to themselves. Now, on her way to Midtown Manhattan, she wondered if these "street people" could possibly be *her* people.

Before the city government developed the area of Times Square, now filled with neon lights, shops, and chain restaurants, the blocks down West Forty-Second Street housed homeless communities and underground businesses. Alternative film companies filled the theater buildings, while groups of people lived outside along the street sidewalks.

Patchwork families of homeless young people lived along the theaters and piers near the water. It was on these blocks that young homeless people often found one another after being pushed out of their childhood homes. Many of Sylvia's soon-to-be friends on Forty-Second Street were also outcast from their families. One by one, Sylvia heard stories that resembled hers. Almost everyone she met had been forced to choose between their home or their truth.

YOUTH HOMELESSNESS IN NEW YORK CITY

Every person has basic needs that help make it possible for them to survive and thrive. These basic needs include shelter and food, yet many young people experience HOUSING and FOOD INSECURITY.

Throughout history, young people have often become homeless as a result of being pushed out of the community they were born into. Looking for help, homeless young people search for others like them. They form communities wherever they can.

It is common for homeless people to be blamed for their situation and then punished. There are high chances of a cycle forming where a homeless person is punished for being homeless, which then makes it harder to find stable ground. For young people, this cycle could be impossible to survive alone.

All people grow up best when they have a stable home, consistent food, and a caring community. While Earth has more than enough natural resources to feed us, people have not found the systems and cooperation to make sure everyone has what they need. Unbalanced resources make it common for some nations and individuals to hoard wealth and for many others to be left with nothing.

But why are so many young people homeless?

When young people experience neglect or a lack of care, they are at high risk of facing homelessness and hunger. Many youth become homeless as a result of their family struggling through poverty generation after generation. Trans and queer young people, from all kinds of families, may be kicked out of their home if their caretakers are unaccepting of their uniqueness.

On the streets, these free-form communities feared being targeted by police. To this day, there remain many laws in place that make it a crime for homeless people to take up space in public. To survive, the community knew they had to stick together and protect one another from violence. Everyone shared what they had learned while living on the street. While they were often only separated by a few years of age, the more experienced community members helped guide the younger, newly arrived ones, like Sylvia. Even with fewer material possessions, this community quickly began to feel like home.

Shortly after arriving at Forty-Second Street, Sylvia was adopted. A fierce and friendly group of older girls cared for Sylvia and eventually took her under their wings. Her chosen family, made of trans women and genderqueer people, nurtured Sylvia in ways her biological family couldn't. Her newfound family taught her how to survive on the streets.

The terms *chosen family* and *houses* traditionally describe underground, queer forms of community, care, and relationship networks. These less-popularized systems of support gave young people like Sylvia a second chance at surviving.

As a preteen, Sylvia wondered what was possible for a girl like her; a girl who had always been told she could only

THE ORIGIN OF HOUSES

Houses are a historical survival tactic and tradition of trans and queer communities. Friends and lovers were looking for words to describe the ways they were caring for one another on the streets, even if they weren't biologically related.

These support structures borrowed language from familial terms. Roles like House MOTHER, House FATHER, SISTER, and more were loosely interpreted and gender expansive. More than just filling a family tree, these relationships were about commitment to helping one another survive.

The house system was formed underground. At the time, it was not possible for queer people to have their relationships and adoption recognized by a court of law. Houses, therefore, included groups of people who chose to stick together, with or without legal paperwork. While houses borrowed the language of nuclear families and played around with the labels, their members were serious about their commitment to support one another.

Ballroom culture was also born underground and created a fun, energetic outlet for communities (and houses) to experience glamour and joy. Balls included competitive and creative challenges, where houses competed to win awards, from dance to design to dress. For trans and queer people of color who experienced layers of discrimination, houses and balls created a subculture of support that helped individuals survive and even have fun.

be a boy. Sylvia's ideas of womanhood had come from the movie stars and fashion models she had seen on magazine covers. Sylvia would watch actresses on-screen and imagine herself in their roles, living out their telenovelas. Now that Sylvia was in the care of people who didn't shame her for exploring her gender, she was free.

Not only was Sylvia safe to explore who she could become, but she was also encouraged to. Like many young trans and queer people before her, feeling safe to explore who she was without expectations or limitations was unlike anything she'd experienced at home; this kind of care and acceptance was life-changing.

Sylvia wasted no time. In addition to now dressing femininely and wearing makeup, her chosen family encouraged her to try out a different name. Sylvia had introduced herself to everyone using the name given to her at birth. While Sylvia didn't necessarily dislike her birth name, she didn't feel connected to it, especially since many people assumed that her name confirmed her boyhood. She liked the idea of getting to choose her own name. For many trans people, choosing a new name can be an important and empowering milestone in their journey toward living authentically. Chosen names, like chosen families, affirm everyone's right to lead their own life.

She chose the name *Sylvia Lee*. Her older trans sisters blessed the moment, and her family celebrated. What Sylvia loved most was how her new name sounded when others said it to call her attention. Unlike the name given to her at birth, *Sylvia Lee Rivera* "just felt right." Her girlfriends encouraged her to use the name permanently, and Sylvia did.

One person that came into Sylvia's life during this time was Marsha "Pay It No Mind" Johnson. Marsha was a street queen and older sister to Forty-Second Street's newer girls. She was a Black trans teenager only a few years older than Sylvia. Like other community members who were only slightly older but had been learning the ways of street life for longer, Marsha became a mentor to Sylvia. The two soon practically became sisters.

One of the first lessons Sylvia learned in her new community was how important it was to stick with your people. Throughout history, people who experienced poverty, homelessness, and other need insecurities have been dismissed, considered a nuisance to the public, targeted, and labeled as vandals and troublemakers. Homelessness is not a crime, and yet, for centuries, lawmakers have passed policies that use vagrancy to justify arresting and removing homeless communities from the public eye. Law enforcement officers have carried out these practices by increasing community policing and targeted arrests.

On top of anti-homeless sentiment, there existed formal and informal practices of policing what clothes people could wear in public. Dress code laws date back to the 1850s and were used to enforce ideas of normative gender. Police followed the "three-piece" rule, which meant that they could arrest people if they weren't wearing at least three pieces of clothing that aligned with the gender on their identification. These

MARSHA P. JOHNSON (1945–1992)

MARSHA P. JOHNSON was one of the mothers of the modern trans and queer liberation movement. Marsha was born on August 24, 1945, in Elizabeth, New Jersey. At an early age, Marsha began to express her desire to dress femininely, having fun in dresses. She quickly experienced backlash for her gender expression and was bullied throughout her childhood years. After Marsha graduated high school, she packed the little she had and moved herself to New York City.

Once she found a community in New York's Greenwich Village, she was free to explore who she was. As a drag queen performer, she first used the name Black Marsha. Later, she changed her name to Marsha P. Johnson. Johnson was from the restaurant name she waitressed at when arriving in Greenwich Village, and the P stood for *pay it no mind*. As a gender-nonconforming person, Marsha would often dismiss questions about her gender, saying, "Pay it no mind." Marsha's dreamy and loving energy made her a beloved mother and sister to many, including Sylvia.

Sylvia and Marsha's sisterhood continued throughout their lives, and they worked together to bring their dream of community into reality. Marsha continues to be honored by the trans and queer community as a role model and, alongside Sylvia, is credited as a mother of the current-day trans, queer, and two-spirit liberation movements.

practices not only intimidated people to follow gender norms, they also gave police officers probable cause to arrest trans and queer people. These rules were used by officers to crash underground masquerades and drag balls where many trans and queer attendees would be dressed in gender-bending attire.

Around Forty-Second Street, New York Police Department (NYPD) officers often sought out trans women and girls and arrested them for not following these restrictive dress codes. In her young years, Sylvia was no stranger to these police encounters.

When Sylvia was arrested for these types of infractions, Viejita would make her way downtown from the Bronx and show up for Sylvia in times of need.

"She always came, bailed me out. [Viejita] says, 'Oh, that's my grandson. I have to take him out.'" Sylvia knew that despite using the word *grandson*, her grandmother was trying.

Later in her life, Sylvia reminisced about how Viejita eventually came around and became more understanding.

"My grandmother completely freaked out for a number of years until she just recently [had] to be satisfied that I'm going to be my way. And now she calls me Sylvia. I'm her dear granddaughter."

The young people on Forty-Second Street were not the only ones experiencing this type of harassment. Following President Eisenhower's 1953 Executive Order 10450, nearly ten thousand queer civil workers were investigated, interrogated, and systemically removed from their government roles. The order claimed queer people were a national security risk. Stemming from the US anti-communist Red Scare, this sweep became known as the Lavender Scare.

State and local laws that enforced strict rules about where people could live, what they could wear, and what work they could take part in meant that people like Sylvia were considered criminals simply for being themselves. But Sylvia refused to accept that and chose to always be herself. *How could being true to herself also mean she deserved to be arrested, over and over again? Had anything changed from getting in trouble at school for defending herself?*

Now that Sylvia could talk to other trans and queer people about her experiences, she began to learn how similar their stories were. Not only did people like her exist, but she also wasn't alone in the struggle. They were all treated the same by a ready-to-reject society.

THE LAVENDER SCARE

After World War II, the US economy was making a comeback through capitalism. Everything that appeared to be anti-capitalist became an "enemy" or "potential threat." Carried out by Senator Joseph McCarthy, MCCARTHYISM was the government's campaign that targeted alleged communists; this time was also known as the Red Scare. Political leaders encouraged civilians to stay alert and report suspicious neighbors.

One of the communities who were framed as likely communist were trans and gay people, then referred to as homosexuals. Before the 1960s, the majority of the trans and queer community was underground and not publicly queer. The Lavender Scare represented a sweeping campaign to remove homosexuals from government office. It was a queer witch hunt.

As the US government grew into a global superpower during the 1900s, political and cultural leaders thought it was important to take seriously how it maintained power. Internationally, American anxiety led to multiple wars with a foreign enemy or potential threat. In the United States, different communities had also been singled out and accused of being internal enemies or potential threats to US power.

The Lavender Scare devastated individual government employees who were fired from their positions, and also instilled fear into the community at large. Beyond firing individual workers, the Red and Lavender Scares were meant to intimidate all people considered suspects.

Sylvia focused her attention on transforming what she was learning into action. Sylvia carried on the tradition of learning all she could from her experiences and sharing what was important, including her new understanding of how the most vulnerable people in society are often the ones taking the brunt of violence. She also saw how Black people around her were being treated. The freedom to be herself was tied up with the freedom of everyone around her. She realized it was all connected. Sylvia even considered why some marginalized people worked so hard to blend in, or assimilate, into mainstream society.

"Actually, you know, at that point in time, I [understood] the ones that held their heads down low, because they probably had very nice jobs and they had a family to go to.

"When you're obvious back then," Sylvia explained, "there was nothing to hold you back."

Imagining a womanhood that included all kinds of women helped to expand Sylvia's ideas of justice. Like many girls—cis and trans—Sylvia was pressured by some to reach for society's ideal of womanhood and try passing as a "real" girl. For trans people, to *pass* meant to blend in with society so well as to be perceived as not being transgender. Not all trans people cared about passing, however, including Sylvia. She refused. Sylvia was not interested in pressuring herself with unrealistic expectations.

Around this time in the 1960s, leaders in the burgeoning feminist rights movement in the United States were engaging in conversations that tried to rebalance gender roles and end violence against all women. However, many feminist cisgender women excluded trans women from the conversation. While some trans women were advocating for their right to be seen as women, Sylvia hesitated to spend too much of her time trying to convince the world of her womanhood. Not only did she care little about passing, but she also felt troubled by the thought of advocating to become part of the unfair power balance between men and women.

WHAT IS THE FEMINIST RIGHTS MOVEMENT?

FEMINISM is the idea of social, economic, and political equality for all people, regardless of gender. Gender has historically been used to categorize and rank people. Men were positioned as the superior gender, while women were structurally made to feel inferior. Women were perceived to be dependent on men and in need of male partnership. Far from an equal exchange, gender has been used to justify domination.

The feminist rights movement describes more than a century of feminists organizing, with multiple waves of change. In the early 1900s, the first wave of feminism focused on women's right to vote and join political discussion. In the 1960s, the second wave worked toward gender equality and the rebalancing of gender roles and power. The feminist third wave throughout the 1990s and early 2000s centered the richness of individualism and diversity. Starting in 2008, the fourth wave of feminism focused on ending gender-based violence. In the 2020s, trans feminism will likely become the next feminist wave, already on its way toward shore.

The second wave of feminism, which Sylvia experienced, was groundbreaking in challenging gender norms in ways that had never been seen before through media and mass mobilizing. Feminists upended the notion that men were superior. This naturally linked to other ways of upending gender roles like queer relationships and genderqueerness.

"I, as a person, don't believe that a transvestite or a woman should do all the wash and do all the cooking and do everything that was forced on by the bourgeois society." Sylvia continued, "That's a whole lot of bologna. If you have a lover or you have a friend that you really care for, you split everything down fifty-fifty."

What began as Sylvia looking to free herself morphed into a vision of liberation of all people. She was not alone in having this vision; these were the issues that were at the center for all young people coming of age at the time.

Supported and taught by her chosen family, Sylvia began to see and understand how the violence she had experienced in her youth was interconnected to the forms of violence others were experiencing. Rather than surrender or give up hope, she was eager to shape change. As the stars would have it, the United States had entered a decade that would witness transformation across many different parts of society.

The 1960s were a pivotal time to grow up and witness the power of community and shared truth. President John F. Kennedy had just been elected, promising the nation "big answers to big questions," as one historian put it following the presidential inauguration on January 20, 1961. Those problems included how big a role the government should play in transforming injustice and inequality both among sexes and genders as well as along racial lines. Americans who were workers, women, and people of color, like Sylvia, were awaiting this support.

But when Vice President Lyndon B. Johnson took over the presidency after Kennedy's assassination in 1963, the promise of a New Frontier was reimagined into Johnson's plans for what he called the "Great Society." In an effort to decrease violence and injustice, Johnson's Great Society intended to give poor people a "hand up, not handout."

WHAT WERE THE NEW FRONTIER AND GREAT SOCIETY?

Leading up to the 1960s, Americans experienced unrest from economic instability and racial violence, both within the United States and globally. The US presidential election was a close race between Democratic nominee John F. Kennedy and Republican nominee Richard Nixon. Lyndon Johnson had lost the Democratic nomination to JFK and joined the Democratic ticket as the vice presidential candidate. What was promised through the campaign closely reflected what was happening in the country at the moment.

After Kennedy's election, the administration pushed forward its plan to secure the economy and bring an end to the escalating racial tension. Called the New Frontier, JFK's plan excited many marginalized communities who believed in his promise for tangible change.

In November 1963, President Kennedy was assassinated while on the campaign trail. JFK's assassination preceded the assassinations of Black leaders Malcolm X (1965) and Martin Luther King Jr. (1968).

Lyndon B. Johnson assumed the presidency and offered his vision of the Great Society. LBJ carried out JFK's goals of civil rights and tax-cut bills passing Congress. Once re-elected, LBJ's agenda toward a Great Society focused on aid to education, medical care, and urban renewal. However, his Wars on Poverty and Crime harmed communities who were hyperpoliced instead of supported and sustained.

Johnson's War on Poverty was a federal government campaign aimed at helping American families escape poverty. Before the campaign had any impact on reducing poverty within the country, the nation's focus turned toward foreign policy. The war happening in Vietnam, Laos, and Cambodia had started in 1955 and was framed to the American public as pro-communist North Vietnam against pro-capitalist South Vietnam.

The United States entered the war in August 1965, motivated by its fear that communism would spread through Asia, which would risk support for a United States–led global economy. The congressional decision for US intervention in the war further divided the nation. In need of soldiers, the US government ordered a draft of eligible Americans. This meant that most young boys and men were required to sign up and start training for war. As gruesome war zone images of Vietnam were printed and televised across the United States, recruits moved into action; some got ready for war, some fled to Canada, and some filled the streets to march against the violence altogether.

At the same time as the Vietnam War, the civil rights movement that was sowed the previous decade grew powerfully across the country. Black leaders like Dr. Martin Luther King Jr. and Malcolm X encouraged all Black and oppressed people to unite and fight toward freedom. The human birthright of self-determination, choosing one's own path and destiny, was core to their message. Congress passed the Civil Rights Act in 1964, which outlawed Jim Crow–era laws that had been used as a way to legalize discrimination against Black people following the abolition of chattel slavery in the mid-1800s.

WHAT ARE JIM CROW LAWS?

When Africans were first brought to the United States, they were documented as enslaved people and considered property, without human rights. In a federal compromise, Black people were counted as three-fifths of a person, in favor of the state's population count. Chattel slavery was legal within the United States through much of the nineteenth century until the 13th Amendment to the Constitution was ratified on December 6, 1963, finally outlawing slavery.

Immediately after the abolition of chattel slavery, Black codes were established to outline how formerly enslaved people could work and how much they were to earn. These codes were meant to be legal loopholes that enforced racial segregation.

JIM CROW LAWS describe laws adopted by state and local governments from the late nineteenth century to the mid-twentieth century. These laws meant to further block Black people from gaining stability or community. Jim Crow laws mandated racial segregation in all public places throughout the Confederate states. The laws were upheld by the Supreme Court decision in *Plessy v. Ferguson*, which stated "separate but equal" was constitutional.

The Voting Rights Act passed the year after the Civil Rights Act, in 1965. Communities of color celebrated these victories as signs of progress, but the policies failed to improve everyday life in Black communities and for other people of color.

Both peace and civil rights movements mobilized masses of people throughout the nation. While violent confrontations between police and protestors filled television screens, community leaders were looking for alternatives and resolutions to conflict without increasing violence. Dr. Martin Luther King Jr. joined peace movement leaders like Buddhist monk Thich Nhat Hanh in calling on people to move toward a beloved community.

By the mid-1960s, Black leaders began to rethink their strategy—if the government was unable and/or unwilling to keep the people safe, the people must keep themselves safe. The Black Panther Party for Self-Defense (BPP) was formed by Bobby Seale and Huey P. Newton in Oakland, California. The Panthers flipped the script: Black power.

THE BLACK PANTHER PARTY FOR SELF-DEFENSE

The BLACK PANTHER PARTY FOR SELF-DEFENSE was an organization started by Huey P. Newton and Bobby Seale, Black students from Merritt College in Oakland, California, in October 1966. The group is often referred to as the Black Panther Party (BPP). BPP learned from and grew out of the civil rights movement. Party leaders took note from the successes and holdups civil rights leaders were experiencing. Although multiple civil rights acts were passed through Congress, the everyday lived experiences of Black people remained unchanged. The Black Panther Party believed that it was time for the community to protect itself.

The BPP introduced a new era to US cultural organizing. The Black Panthers' vision was summed up in their Ten-Point Program platform that outlines their demands for Black power: *Self-determination. Employment. End to capitalism. Housing. Education. No forced military service. End police brutality. Freedom from prison. Trial by peers. Peace.*

Their mission was transformed into community-based resources including breakfast programs for children, community ambulances, and more. BPP spread throughout the nation and peaked in membership with five thousand members in 1969. The BPP style of dress and organizing attracted many young people into action, including non-Black communities. As their numbers grew, the government feared the influence of the Black Panther Party. It was soon infiltrated and demolished by the US government. BPP leaders were considered internal enemies and potential threats to US power.

In New York City, students, street people, and many community members organized massive demonstrations that demanded *all power to the people*. The Young Lords were a Chicago-based street gang that moved with the vision of a political organization protecting the self-determination of Puerto Ricans, Latinx people, and other third world peoples. Sylvia often joined actions alongside the Young Lords' NYC chapter, although she did not become an official member.

These visionary community-rooted groups, and their focus on peace and justice, instilled in Sylvia a commitment to creating a sense of beloved community that all people felt welcomed and supported by. Because street people, many of whom were also people of color, had experienced state violence from police, public officials, and the military, they joined the front lines of many public demonstrations. Putting their bodies on the line for peace and civil rights made sense for the trans and queer people who knew exactly what being targeted for simply existing felt like.

The support and solidarity street people offered these social justice movements, however, was not always reciprocated. Within the wider trans and queer community, queer street people were often devalued and outcast. This left them asking, "Why are the people who claim to be advocating for peace and civil rights not willing to extend their vision to include us?"

As the decade continued, trans and queer people

dreamed of freedom that included everyone, regardless of who they were or who they loved. And using what they learned from other social movements, they began to fight back any chance they got.

One night in August 1966, in the Tenderloin District of San Francisco, drag queens and queer community members stood up against the constant police harassment they faced while hanging out at Compton's Cafeteria. Gene Compton's was a popular spot where queens and queers would gather after a long night out. When San Francisco police officers attempted to detain some patrons without cause, salt shakers and other items were flung through the air. More uprisings like that at Compton's sparked in the late 1960s as queer people began to openly resist their oppressors. It was only a matter of time until the action came home to Sylvia in New York City.

CHAPTER THREE

QUEENS RIDE TO BATTLE

Sylvia was no longer alone in her struggle. By the end of the 1960s, she had created a community with many other trans and queer teens who had also come from unloving homes but were determined to survive.

After a few years on Forty-Second Street, Sylvia, like others before her, began mentoring girls who arrived after her. Everyone in Sylvia's community protected one another, which also made it possible for them to . . . have fun! When they could find a safe place for everyone to relax together, the community rejoiced. With what little they had, they used their creativity and energy to make it work.

Dominant cultures have historically maintained power by controlling the ways in which individuals are allowed to be themselves. Subcultures that have been unable to defend themselves are often forced to seek refuge behind closed doors, or underground. Even under this pressure and risk, many oppressed groups refuse to throw away the parts of themselves that are core to who they are. They find ways to protect their spirit and escape surveillance. Activities that engage the body—like dancing, singing, and art—have often provided these kinds of healing outlets. These practices offer oppressed people a way to strengthen hope and, when the moment is right, to rise up against their oppressors.

In New York City, law enforcement had long been weaponized against poor and queer people of color. Dating back to the 1850s, police followed an informal rule that made it a crime for people to wear clothing of a different gender than they were assigned at birth. The "three-piece" rule meant that one could be arrested if they didn't have at least three pieces of clothing that matched the gender on their ID card. These state practices intimidated the public to follow gender norms and gave police officers the probable cause to arrest. Sylvia and thousands of other trans and queer street people were often arrested for wearing the "wrong" clothes in public spaces.

Young trans and queer kids didn't take this abuse quietly. Determined to live the lives Sylvia and others left home for, they chose freedom over obedience.

Dance clubs and underground ballrooms provided a

refuge for trans and queer people to relax and have fun. The Stonewall Inn was a queer bar in the heart of New York City's Greenwich Village, where members of the community came to dance and hang out. Places like Stonewall were well known to the trans and queer communities who frequented them but were often disguised from the public and law enforcement. They were a break from the outside world. The Stonewall Inn was one of these places where the community could connect and party as their true selves.

Ironically, gay male bouncers did not always allow the feminine queers and drag queens into Stonewall. The nicer spaces that existed at the time often catered to white gay men with money, which left trans people, poor queers, and people of color out. Sylvia and other street queers were thought to be classless by this part of their community. Well versed in how to deal with exclusion, Sylvia and her friends found their way in.

"You could get into the Stonewall if they knew you and there were only a certain amount of drag queens that were allowed into the Stonewall at that time," Sylvia recounted.

Whether or not all queer people were allowed in, the Stonewall was viewed by the Mafia and NYPD as easy bait—both for money and arrests.

The Stonewall, like many queer bars, was operating under multiple layers of manipulated power. The bar was owned and run by members of the Mafia, who negotiated illegal deals with the NYPD. In exchange for cash payouts, officers would not always arrest the bar owners for selling bootleg liquor. Many bars throughout the 1960s were actually small private clubs that skipped over city licenses and inspections. At the Stonewall and other queer bars, if payouts were not given, the patrons were at risk of arrest since it was illegal for queer people to be seen in public together. Sometimes, the Mafia would allow for the arrest of some of patrons in order to pay the balance on their debt to the NYPD.

"This is what we learned to live with," Sylvia would recall. The only loyalty people had was to profit.

Before the Black Panthers, justice movements were expected to resist violence in nonviolent, dignified, and bureaucratic ways. The goal of respectable organizing was to prove that oppressed people could fit into the oppressor's system. The Compton's Cafeteria uprising in San Francisco in 1966 was an example of trans and queer people openly resisting state violence, fighting back against police discrimination regardless of how they might be perceived. They boldly refused to be taken easily. So when NYPD officers decided to arrest everyone inside the Stonewall one night in June 1969, the moment had arrived for queers and queens in New York City to fight back.

Sylvia had been waiting for this.

"It was, like, a godsent thing," Sylvia said. "I just happened to be there when it all jumped off. I said, 'Well, great. Now it's my time.' Here, I'm out there being a revolutionist for everybody else. I said, 'Now it's time to do my thing for my own people.'"

On Tuesday, June 24, 1969, the NYPD Public Moral Division raided the Stonewall. The patrons were removed, liquor confiscated, and staff arrested. One of the bar owners made it clear to inspector Seymour Pine that the Stonewall would be back to business the next day. He kept his promise. And so Inspector Pine returned once more that weekend—this time he brought backup. The patrons were used to these raids since they happened almost weekly. The routine was as follows:

1. NYPD arrives.
2. The officers take all the alcohol and their payoff.

3. Officers leave and bolt the door, having maybe arrested a few people.
4. After fifteen minutes, bar owners break the bolt and reopen.

After midnight on June 28, the lights suddenly went on at the Stonewall Inn; another police raid had begun. But on this night, the payoff wasn't enough.

The room froze when NYPD announced the raid would continue. Their new plan that night: take the alcohol, cash, and arrest anyone in the bar without proper ID and clothing. In a queer crowd, the chances of someone's government ID not matching their appearance is high, which meant many patrons were about to be arrested.

"I wasn't in full drag," Sylvia remembered. "I was dressed, you know, very pleasantly. I was wearing a woman's suit. Bell-bottoms were out then. I had made this fabulous suit at home, and I was wearing that and I had the hair out. Lots of makeup, lots of hair!"

The officers ordered the crowd to divide into three groups: men, women, and "others." The police officers checked people's clothing and ID as they exited. Trans and genderqueer people without ID or the "proper" clothing were held in the coatroom. Inside the closet, tension was rising among friends who knew they were going to jail. Sylvia began to wonder: *Why are we forced to accept this treatment?*

The patrons who had been released waited outside the Stonewall for their friends to be let go. Across the street from the Stonewall was a small park where groups hung out at as they waited. Each time someone came out the doors, they were met with a cheering crowd. Amid the uncertainty, the energy of those small moments was electrifying.

Then community members who had been detained were led outside and loaded into the police wagon. According to Sylvia, there was a moment in the chaos when the air around them stilled and everyone realized what was about to happen.

"I don't know if it was the customers or it was the police. It just . . ." Sylvia snapped her fingers. "Everything clicked."

Nickels, dimes, and quarters started flying toward the officers. The crowd shouted "Payoff!" as they tossed the coins. *NYPD already had taken their money, why were they still taking our people?* As frustration intensified among the crowd, the coins gave way to heavy objects.

Those arrested in handcuffs took the opportunity and

began to resist. Their friends who had waited outside let open the doors of the police wagon. Quickly the crowd realized what was happening and joined in as handcuffed queens disappeared into the crowd. The situation flipped on the officers who started the raid.

Coins turned into rocks and parking meters. Windows were smashed and trash cans set on fire. Inspector Pine and his squad retreated back inside the bar to take shelter.

Outside, the crowd grew in size, energy, and fury. The more-than-forty Stonewall patrons were now joined by hundreds of people. They called in friends, neighbors, and passersby from the surrounding bars and apartment buildings. For the queer people who were familiar with police brutality, the energy was irresistible.

"It was a dramatic gesture of defiance."

When one person threw a rock and shattered one of the second-floor windows of the Stonewall Inn, the crowd let out a mesmerized *oooooh*.

At one point, an officer opened the door and pointed their gun toward the crowd with an order for everyone to disperse. But the crowd refused. With the cops locked inside the bar, people in the crowd stayed for hours. Some even went home to rest and return right after. Knowing officers were trapped, Inspector Pine called in the Tactical

Patrol Force (TPF). The TPF was known throughout the community as the city's army in times of civil unrest. Armed with military-grade weapons, TPF rolled in and pushed the mob back.

A chorus line of queens started to kick their heels at the cops and sang, "We are the Village girls / We wear our hair in curls / We wear our dungarees / Above our nellie knees / And when it comes to boys / We simply hypnotize—"

The song was cut short when TPF charged in their direction. *Chaos.*

Fights between TPF officers and community members broke out. Cars were turned over. Traffic was blocked and people were screaming. The crowd was pushed back toward Seventh Avenue but split in two, moving around the small Village blocks. For a short time, the crowd was amused by the parade-like chase, but all distractions ended when tear gas was used on the rioters, forcing everyone to leave the area.

After the first night of protests, thirteen people had been arrested. The few people who hung out around the Village as the sun came up collected pieces from the night's scene. Broken glass shimmered across the ground, and the smell of garbage-can fires still filled the air.

The *Village Voice*, a New York City newspaper, criticized the community for fighting back against NYPD and TPF but also noted how the altercation with a group of queers was difficult for officers to control. This was a turning point in the attitudes of trans and queer people who now saw their individual and collective strength.

That night, a crowd gathered in front of the Stonewall, reinvigorated. Chants where yelled while garbage cans were set on fire. Police officers returned to the scene and cleared out the crowd once more, only for them to show up again the next night.

The Stonewall uprisings lasted for six days.

Before Stonewall, the lived experiences of trans and queer people were usually restricted to nightlife, hidden away and kept secret. The Stonewall uprising, along with the media attention it received, created a cultural shift in what it meant to be queer. No longer would the trans and queer community silently experience these unfair abuses of power. It was time to be out, loud, and proud.

Stonewall transformed a spark into a movement.

The revolution was here.

After news of the Stonewall uprisings had spread nationally, queer communities were no longer trying to live in the closet. It was time for their people to be able to step out of the shadows. Visibility brought questions. *Who are we? Who am I?* These were similar questions that feminists and civil rights leaders were reflecting on through the 1960s. Now that trans and queer people were breaking isolation and storytelling, space surfaced for the community to put language to the truth they had long felt.

The cultural shift that brought queerness into the public eye opened the doors to many possibilities. For the first time on such a large scale, queer people were openly devising freedom. Stars were beginning to shine.

CHAPTER FOUR

FALLING STARS

After the Stonewall uprisings, trans and queer people were eager to continue momentum. No longer were they on the sidelines of action, they were leading. The uprisings did not change how NYPD engaged with community members, but they had emboldened trans and queer people longing for freedom.

What the uprisings made clear was that trans and queer people had the power to defend themselves and their community against anyone who tried to harm them. No longer would queer people be kept in the shadows and silenced. It was time for the community to be "Out and Proud!"

There was a wave of community members who now saw their coming-out as a political act, encouraged by the public perception toward queer people. To openly identify as queer was a risk, but it felt necessary to push societal change. For the first time, friends who lived openly encouraged the queer people in their lives to do the same. If there was power in numbers, queer people knew they needed everyone they could gather.

Groups of queer people across the country mobilized into action. Those who had been involved in anti-war and civil rights organizing now joined queer-focused organizations.

Openly queer organizing allowed people to bring their full selves into their advocacy. Whereas before it was expected to advocate for peace and racial justice without alluding to queerness, feminist and queer activists helped to bring gender into the conversation of freedom. Queer people challenged the medically accepted diagnosis that queerness was a mental illness. Learning from feminists who asserted and protected their own sanity when called anything less, queer people followed suit.

This radical shift in visibility helped the queer community enter into national dialogue. Within the community, a lifetime of keeping their identity hidden from the public eye had come to an end.

The Stonewall uprisings were a coming-out. And one thing was certain: the community must hold their ground.

Prior to the Stonewall uprisings, the Mattachine Society and Daughters of Bilitis were two secret groups for politically active gay and lesbian people, respectively. Both of these organizations formed over a decade before the 1969 uprisings and functioned mostly underground throughout the 1950s and '60s.

In the weeks following Stonewall, New York City activists from the Mattachine Society and Daughters of Bilitis organized themselves into the Mattachine Action Committee. While Mattachine and Bilitis were run by older queer leaders, the action committee was led by radical young activists ready to come out from underground who nudged the Mattachine and Bilitis leaders to pay attention to what was happening in the streets.

Co-leader Martha Shelley and other members of the committee were ready for action and wanted to call for a march. So they did.

On July 29, 1969, only a month after the uprisings, over five hundred people gathered outside the Stonewall and marched down Christopher Street. There were reports of the march's peak attendance being approximately two thousand marchers.

By the end of 1969, New York City activists formed a new, widely inclusive group called Gay Liberation Front (GLF). The group name was inspired by the liberation army of North Vietnam, the National Liberation Front of

North Vietnam, which was made of Vietnamese peasants "daring to stand up against the most powerful army in the world." In this spirit, GLF welcomed all community members and allies to join forces for gay (queer) liberation. The group's vision for justice was not only inclusive of gay identity but also considered all genders, ethnicities, and class backgrounds. After a decade of many single-issue movements, it made sense to GLF leadership that the group's vision include liberation for everyone as the goal.

Practicing their vision proved more difficult than imagined. While it was easy to know who was on their

MARTHA SHELLEY

MARTHA SHELLEY was born in Brooklyn, New York, on December 27, 1943, to Russian Polish Jewish parents. An activist, a writer, and a poet, Martha is recognized as one of the leaders of the lesbian feminist movement, serving as president for the Daughters of Bilitis and making up part of the group of approximately twenty people who formed the Gay Liberation Front following the Stonewall riots.

side and who wasn't during the protests, sticking together over time was challenging. Smaller groups within GLF fractured off as political differences put pressure on the group's unity. Young people under twenty-one years of age were not allowed to join GLF, a precautionary step by the older queer leaders who wanted to avoid the group being accused of converting children. This led young people to form their own group, called Gay Youth (GY), and begin to organize their own spaces, events, and politics. GY became a community hub for young gay kids, mostly gay boys, throughout the city.

Radicalesbians was another GLF seed group, led by gay women. Lesbian leaders spoke to the layered impacts of both homophobia and sexism. Community members who wished to solely focus on liberation for gay men formed Gay Activists Alliance (GAA). GAA was led mostly by middle-class gay white men.

Sylvia and other street queens wanted to stay connected to the various groups but were met with some resistance when none of the factions welcomed them.

One afternoon, Sylvia and her friends called GAA leaders and inquired if the group welcomed queens. None of them identified as men, but they were curious to see how accepting the space was.

"I was there when GAA first started, four months, when it was four months old," said Sylvia in a 1989 interview. "I made a phone call from Jersey and said, 'Do you accept transvestites?' At that time, I was still using the word 'drag queen.' I said, 'Do you accept drag queens?' 'Sure, come on down.'"

So, they "tipped down there to the meeting from Jersey, and [they] walk in, [they] took a peek, and it was nothing but butch male homosexuals that always oppressed transvestites."

But that didn't stop them.

"We were very flamboyant with the makeup and everything, you know, tipping in, you know, really looking . . . beautiful. So, like, we walked away. We walked up the block and we came back and we peeked in some more. I said, 'No, let's go home.' We walked about five blocks. I said, 'No. Let's go in and freak them out for the hell of it.'" *Nothing* stopped Sylvia.

When the group of friends walked in, they were asked to sign in.

"What's your name?"

"My name is Sylvia."

"What is your name?"

Sylvia repeated, "I'm Sylvia!"

But the GAA representative refused. "Well, we can't accept that name."

Upset and determined, Sylvia wrote down her chosen name, but included her given name next to it. Even though she guessed she may not be welcome, she hoped for a possibility.

"I wrote down 'Sylvia Lee Rivera,' but in parentheses I have the habit of putting 'Ray Rivera,' my real name. Even butch-identified, even men, you know, homosexual males that are dealing with their sexism are always discriminating against transvestites because they just can't . . . We're threatening their masculinity. That's the way they feel."

The request for "real names" was meant to embarrass the girls, but they walked in anyway and took their seats. *After all, where else were they going to go?*

The multiple organizations across the city continued to work together as they figured out a strategy. The coalition set their eyes on fighting for legal recognition and protection from violence. In a similar way civil rights groups had demanded to be seen as equal under US law, queer groups demanded policy change from their representatives.

One of the first campaigns that New York City–based groups focused on was Intro 475, city ordinance that proposed to ban discrimination of queer people. Leaders knew that in order for queer people to be protected under law, lawmakers would need to believe queer identities and extend legal protections to the group. GLF groups set out to garner support for the policy.

Sylvia joined the campaign to help pass Intro 475. She worked her way through the neighborhood and collected signatures in support of the bill. Every person she talked to was also encouraged to join the activism. Through her past organizing for peace and civil rights, Sylvia had learned how important unified communities and relationships were. People power requires a lot of people!

When Sylvia was petitioning for signatures in April 1970 on Forty-Second Street, local police officers told Sylvia she was not allowed to petition. With stacks of signed petitions in hand, Sylvia didn't back down. She insisted it was within her rights to collect signatures and refused to stop.

"The cops came up to me and [said], 'No, no, no, no, you can't do this. Either you leave or we're going to arrest you.' I said, 'Well, fine, arrest me.' They very nicely picked me up and threw me in a police car and took me to jail," Sylvia explained.

These moments made it clear to others how dedicated Sylvia was to the work, and her community was dedicated to her. Many filled the courtroom audience during Sylvia's case hearing about a month after her arrest to show the judge the strong community she was a part of. After reviewing the case, the preceding judge said, "The whole country is in an uproar and you're messing with a person circulating a petition?" and quickly dropped the charges. Once out of jail, Sylvia went back to collecting signatures.

Leading up to June 1970, community leaders were focused on organizing a march for the one-year anniversary of the Stonewall uprisings. The GLF action committee formally voted to change the annual Reminder Day to Christopher Street Liberation Day (CSLD). Reminder Day had been an annual picket organized by the Mattachine Society every Fourth of July at Independence Hall. While Reminder Day was meant to remind the public that queer people were not being given their constitutional rights, it sparked tension within the community when event organizers asked the crowd to act respectable, or "less queer."

Christopher Street Liberation Day, on the other hand, was a message to the world that queer people were not ashamed of who they are. In fact, they were *proud*. Since being openly queer in public was still considered a crime, the choice to march was bold and felt necessary.

At the same time as organizers were planning for

CSLD, queer-led protests, newspapers, and organizations were sparking everywhere. When the pride march organizers applied for a permit, it was rejected. The NYPD kept its eyes on what was happening. The planning committee were instead called into a meeting at the NYPD third division headquarters. The meeting included lieutenants, inspectors, and servants from the department. Even Inspector Pine, who led the raid on Stonewall, sat across the table from the committee.

The department asked their questions and reviewed the planned route. The event organizers asked whether officers planned to arrest people who dressed in clothes that did not match the gender on their ID. NYPD's reply was that the information couldn't be shared, so the event's organizers were kept in the dark.

Without approval, the CSLD committee continued on. Organizers in other cities also worked on bringing the CSLD march to their city. Chicago and San Francisco activists organized marches that summer.

On June 28, 1970, thousands gathered near West Washington Place, just a few blocks from where the Stonewall uprisings took place the year before. They marched through the streets holding hands, chanting, and having fun. They chanted, "P! O! W! E! R! Gay power!"

Sylvia and other trans people marched together as a group alongside Gay Youth toward the front of the fifteen-block procession.

Organizers had not expected such a turnout, but their goal was accomplished; their work had guaranteed that the uprisings in June 1969 would not be lost to history.

By September 1970, at nineteen years old, Sylvia was homeless again. The dedication and effort she put into the movement had not helped her escape poverty.

While sleeping in Sheridan Square park, Sylvia was spotted by Bob Kohler, a supportive older gay activist who had helped launch GLF. He was on his way to New York University (NYU) to support a group of students who were in the middle of a sit-in protest. Student-led protests had become common in the 1960s and continued into the 1970s.

Bob shared what he knew about what was happening at NYU and why. He told Sylvia how the queer students were demanding support from their campus administration by taking over the basement of a campus building. Columbia University students, across the city, had also organized an action in support of gay rights the year prior. Bob warned that the action may get intense, but Sylvia, who was the average age of most university students, followed him anyway.

The student sit-in took place in the basement of NYU's Weinstein Hall to protest a denied event permit and the campus's lack of support for trans and queer students. Multiple community-based groups gathered in solidarity with NYU's Gay Student Liberation. Those present included members of Gay Liberation Front, Christopher Street Liberation Day committee, Radicalesbians, Gay Activist Alliance, and Gay Youth.

Sylvia joined the crowd of demonstrators, mixed with both students and community members. There were also some of Sylvia's friends from her street community. The sit-in was an opportunity for different people to exchange stories about their experiences on campus or while living in the street. Conversation filled the hours of the multiple days they occupied Weinstein Hall. Storytelling helped highlight the similar experiences, while also making clear the parts of their stories that were unique.

The exchange between community members deepened their understanding of each other and themselves. The conversations inside Weinstein Hall were one of the first times that Sylvia and other trans people tried to put words to their experiences with gender. At the time, trans girls and queens were still thought of as super-feminine gay men, which wasn't their truth. Yes, trans people experienced homophobia and discrimination for being read as queer, but there was more to their stories. There had always been more to the experiences of queer people who also transcended gender lines and roles. Finally, those long-silenced stories were being spoken aloud.

Not only did the protest bring a sense of self-discovery, but it also underlined other key issues experienced by many trans community members. The differences in experience between trans people and non-trans gay men raised the question of how to honor the unique parts of each community's experience. The high rates of trans young people who made up local homeless populations pointed to how urgent the needs for stable housing and basic needs were. Having access to the temporary housing of an NYU basement also reminded the group how urgent of an issue poverty was.

Encouraged by the energy that filled the NYU building basement, Sylvia and other trans street people spoke their truth: *Transvestites for gay power!* At the time, *transvestite* was the term that felt closest to describing their gender experience. *Transgender* would not be used as a label for decades to come.

On September 25, four days after the sit-in began, activists were forcibly removed by the city's Tactical Patrol Force—the same militarized force called in during the Stonewall uprisings. Although the protest ended, its impact offered a new perspective for Sylvia and other street trans people. Following the Weinstein Hall demonstration, Sylvia, Marsha, and their friends continued to attend and organize rallies as the newly self-proclaimed group STAR: Street Transvestite Action Revolutionaries.

The naming of trans existence and founding of STAR felt liberating and full of potential. In the same way the community had called for gay liberation, and similar to the smaller groups beginning to create space for themselves within GLF's vision, STAR was coming to life on its own.

REVOLUTION OF TRANS TERMINOLOGY

Throughout history, we've seen how humanity changes and evolves, and how with some of that change also comes a shift in language. After all, if you went back one hundred years and asked to borrow a smartphone, they would be very confused. *(How can phones be smart?)*

Similarly, TRANS TERMINOLOGY has evolved over time, and more recent terms have done so in relation to our understanding of biological sex, gender identity, and gender expression. Today, we use the word *transgender*, which reinforces the difference between gender and sex. Before that, the word used was *transsexual*, which focused on the change of one's biological sex. And before that it was *transvestite*, which is what they called people who dressed in clothes that were marketed for the other gender.

As norms surrounding gender and sex continue to change, and our understanding of them increases, it's possible that trans terminology will continue evolving, staying in flux as our society also changes and evolves.

The group went into action.

A month after the Weinstein Hall sit-in, STAR organized a rolling protest with multiple stops at Bellevue Hospital, the NYU campus, and NYPD headquarters. Each stop along the march's route were sites where STAR members had experienced ongoing incidents of gender-based discrimination. Bellevue, NYU, and NYPD were all places that were thought to serve the community but had refused to treat trans people as equal human beings.

Later that year, STAR worked with GLF, Radicalesbians, Gay Youth, and Third World Gay Revolution to launch and sustain the Gay Community Center (GCC). The GCC was based in a shared, local NYC apartment, and it was used as a safe social space. The GCC often held classes and discussion groups as well as other activities that helped the queer community as they navigated the world around them.

STAR's collective and growing group empowerment at times created tension within the post-Stonewall queer community. While STAR tried to stretch the movement's shared vision of liberation to include issues their members faced, the strategy among other groups focused on gaining acceptance from the wider, heteronormative society. Issues like housing and food insecurity, random or targeted arrests, and violence were not prioritized. With their goal of having queer people accepted into society, some gay and lesbian leaders were uncomfortable with the complex and layered experiences of trans people. These leaders had always thought of street people and trans people as distractions and obstacles in the work. They worried STAR and its bold leaders lessened the community's chances of blending in.

Trying to be compassionate about their anxieties, Sylvia took every opportunity to remind her people that equality should not come at the expense of a part of the community. Sylvia was relentless in her belief that everyone deserved to be free. She didn't budge as she developed a reputation as a fiery queen. In her mind, what others thought about her was less important than doing what was needed to keep trans people alive, thriving, and fighting for liberation.

Sylvia and Marsha P. Johnson knew that the community sustaining itself was the only way toward lasting livelihood. Unsure whether gay and lesbian groups in the community would ever prioritize trans youth, Sylvia and Marsha knew they had to create care networks themselves. They set out to do just that: securing a place to call home where everyone could be cared for.

Sylvia knew that if STAR could secure a physical

place, her people had a chance at making it possible. For generations, trans people who left unsupportive families had created families of their own, much like Sylvia had done when she was only ten years old. The connections homeless trans youth made with each other were validating, but even with each other, surviving on the street was close to impossible. Sylvia and Marsha dreamed of what they would call their future home: STAR House.

Throughout their teenage years on Forty-Second Street, the two sisters daydreamed about all the places they would visit in the future together. Although it might have seemed unrealistic for two homeless teens to travel across the world, imagination helped to give each of them something to live for. Soon, daydreams transformed into promises. Daydreams became the lights at the end of their tunnel.

They dreamed about the River Jordan—a river that travels from the mouth of the Dead Sea and touches Jordan, Israel, Syria, and Palestine. In Jewish and Christian traditions, the River Jordan holds great meaning, often referring back to moments of newfound freedom and rebirth.

"You're not crossing the River Jordan without me," Marsha made clear to Sylvia.

Before crossing the Jordan, Sylvia and Marsha had more immediate dreams to pursue. *Where could they live that night . . . and the next day . . . and the next?*

As acting mothers for their slightly younger street kids, Sylvia and Marsha taught their children the value of community. They knew how important it was for young people to be able to rely on one another to survive each day. Solidarity and community had kept both Sylvia and Marsha alive for nearly ten years. STAR's potential relied on the wider gay community showing up in support, similar to the ways STAR members had shown up to support other community movements.

As STAR continued organizing, Sylvia and Marsha began to save their money. While they fundraised for an apartment, Sylvia, Marsha, and almost twenty other young people made a temporary home in the back of a trailer truck.

After cosponsoring a dance fundraiser with GLF, STAR members had enough money for an apartment on Second Street in Greenwich Village. The apartment was owned by members of the Mafia, just like the Stonewall Inn. The apartment was run-down and required a lot of work to become habitable. Everyone within the family pitched in to get the house ready for move-in.

STAR House opened in November 1970. House mothers Sylvia and Marsha provided a home to around twenty other young street people, all rotating and growing within the apartment's four rooms. For the first time in a decade, Sylvia had a home.

As soon as everyone was able to eat and get used to living in a home again, STAR members began to feel energized for more activism. While the young people were usually ready to join in action, they had been doing so without consistent housing or food. Many of these kids had not received stable care and resources for years.

STAR hosted community meetings in the house occasionally. Everyone was welcomed, including non-trans members of GAA and GY. STAR House became an example of what is possible when trans and queer youth are given the care they need to survive and thrive. Unlike gay and lesbian leaders, STAR was not concerned about blending into society. Most of the people who were part of STAR knew that they were nowhere close to being welcomed into the "straight world." While they often fantasized about life as seen on fashion magazines full of beautiful, carefree models, the group's priority was to end violence against their people. Now that they had a home, and had filled it with everyone that could fit, STAR focused its energy on helping free their people from jail.

In January 1971, STAR and other activist groups formed the Gay Community Prison Committee to publicly investigate the violence trans and queer people were experiencing in jail. Within a few months, however, support for their committee work and small organization began to dwindle. In July, Sylvia got word from the house's landlord that Bubbles, the STAR House member responsible for paying rent, hadn't been paying. Nine months after opening and unable to backpay, STAR House was evicted.

STAR House's closing led to the reality that Sylvia and Marsha had worked hard to prevent. Marsha moved back into her old apartment, which resumed its role as STAR's default headquarters. Sylvia stayed with friends. Some STAR House members found places to crash. Others headed back to Forty-Second. Unfortunately, some house members eventually lost their lives to street violence.

"When we asked the community to help us, there was nobody to help us. We were nothing. We were nothing!" Sylvia cried. "We were taking care of kids that were younger than us. I mean, Marsha and I were young, and we were taking care of them.

"GAA had teachers and lawyers and whatnot and all we asked them was, well, if you could help us teach our own so we can all become a little bit better. There was nobody there to help us. There was nobody."

Meanwhile, conservative political leaders strategized their nationwide response to interrupt the steady rise in visible queerness across the country. The concept of "traditional family values" was created to promote Christian values. These idealized standards were weaponized against interracial and same-gender couples whose relationships were accused of damaging the country's moral fabric. Some gay and lesbian leaders tried to mold their

WHAT WERE CONSERVATIVE LEADERS DOING AT THE TIME?

The United States throughout the twentieth century focused on holding its position as a global superpower. Insecure of their power, US leaders moved with determination and aggression. By the 1960s, the United States had consumed small countries like Hawaii and had entered the Vietnam War.

Within the United States, conservative leaders strategically divided the country. Using red-lining strategies and moral panic, leaders took advantage of community division in order to maintain their power. The concept of traditional family values was used to easily differentiate people who fit the model nuclear family (mostly upper- and middle-class white people) from all other people and communities. The idea of a nuclear family and traditional family values were raised to create more rigid models of acceptable lifestyles. By promoting what was considered traditional family values, alternative forms of life that didn't align with white America were seen as nontraditional, other, or inferior. Caregiving within communities of color and queer relationships was critiqued under this mindset.

groups to fit these conservative fairy tales. Eager to assimilate into society's masses, gay and lesbian communities began to remove trans people from the shared vision of gay liberation. The revolutionary vision and spirit of the Stonewall uprisings started to crack under the pressure to conform into a palatable narrative.

Where are our gay brothers and sisters? Sylvia was asking herself as STAR House faced eviction and closed. Sylvia and STAR continued to support all gay movements and organizations but were increasingly upset at the lack of mutual support. Over the years, it became clear that community priorities had shifted. While STAR was focused on keeping unhoused and underfed young people alive and out of jail, gay and lesbian advocates focused on civil rights at work and school. But most STAR members had neither steady employment nor education. Sylvia urged gay and lesbian activists to keep trans people and homeless queers in their work, yet deep down knew she was talking to people that weren't listening.

The concern that trans people would be pushed out of the liberation movement was confirmed when gay leaders agreed to a compromise with city politicians in their work to pass Intro 475. Behind closed doors, trans people were edited out when organizers agreed to drop gender discrimination from Intro 475's legal protections. In December 1971, when Intro 475 was up for vote, with trans people removed from the bill's protection, it still did not pass. Pass or fail, the sacrifice that had been made was clear.

The divide between community groups widened over the next year. Once united in a vision of interconnected liberation, some gay and lesbian groups continued to tighten their tone. Lesbian leaders voiced their discomfort with trans women and drag queens impersonating women for fun or entertainment

Event organizers of the fourth-annual Christopher Street Liberation Day tried to smooth tensions between organizations in June 1973. Their goal was to maintain the event's focus on celebrating the community's pride. The planning committee limited the speaking list and chose speakers they thought were neutral to political divides among the community.

Before the rally, members of Lesbian Feminist Liberation (LFL) dispersed flyers that mocked drag queens and compared their entertainment to STAR members' trans identities. Trans people were being thrown under the bus even before the event began—the same event that celebrated uprisings led by trans people just a few years prior.

Sylvia was determined to have her words heard.

Sylvia fought her way through the crowd. She was hit and pulled away from the stage but continued on. Eventually she made it onto the stage. Sylvia grabbed the hands of emcee Vito Russo and wrestled the microphone away from him. Exhausted, she took a minute to catch her breath. She had something to say, and these people—*her* people—were going to hear it.

While onstage, Sylvia spoke about the countless times trans people experienced violence without any support from gay and lesbian people. "Do you do anything for them? No!" Sylvia yelled. "You all tell me, go and hide my tail between my legs. I will no longer put up with this!" Full of emotion and exhaustion, her speech concluded:

[Trans] people are trying to do something for all of us, and not men and women that belong to a white middle-class white club. And that's what you all belong to!
REVOLUTION NOW! Gimme a *G*! Gimme an *A*! Gimme a *Y*! Gimme a *P*! Gimme an *O*! Gimme a *W*! Gimme an *E*! Gimme an *R*! [crying] Gay power! Louder! GAY POWER!

Jean O'Leary, leader of LFL, hopped onstage to remind the crowd of LFL's transphobic views. Activist Lee Brewster in full drag then grabbed the mic to correct O'Leary's claims. Lee set the record straight and reminded the crowd of what drag queens did at Stonewall to advance the fight that led to the Liberation Day celebration.

In the years following, the gay liberation organizations

and their leaders continued to pull back their vision: The movement's direction moved from liberation to assimilation. Without trans people in leadership anymore, the movement that had set out to be queer and free was getting further from both.

CHAPTER FIVE

LOOKING FOR MY SISTERS

The momentum that the Stonewall uprisings created began to slow down as political disagreement within the community deepened. The revolutionary energy was fading.

The question regarding queer people's rights had entered into the public eye, causing gay and lesbian leaders to feel pressured to maintain the community's chances of being accepted into society by molding their people into the ideal citizens; and leaders used this pressure to justify distancing the movement from those who would be considered unrespectable.

For this reason, homeless transgender people were seen by community leaders as threats to the community's potential, feeling that gay and lesbian civil rights were closer to recognition but were being held back by trans issues and leaders. Much like political leaders in government, gay and lesbian leaders saw people like Sylvia and her children as issues that needed to be dealt with. As a result of the hostility, the same street queens who were on the front lines for most uprisings were now being pushed out of the movement entirely. At the core of what kept trans people and their politics together was usually a shared desire to live and immediate need for community care, but in exiling them from the wider community, lesbian and gay leaders were causing harm. Ultimately, the choice to outcast trans individuals was strategic.

After the 1973 Liberation Day rally, at twenty-two years old, Sylvia felt hopeless. For more than ten years, Sylvia's deep love for her community sustained her fierce passion and work. She had studied the techniques of older leaders and put her body on the line over and over because she had nothing more important to sacrifice.

Sylvia's experience of being beat up while making her way to the Liberation Day stage, being booed and hit by people in the crowd, was proof that there was little chance for change: The community she depended on would not show up for her when she needed it to. This devastated and exhausted Sylvia and led her into despair. After the march, Sylvia harmed herself and required medical care to survive.

Thankfully, she wasn't truly alone. Marsha, who had

followed a feeling in her gut telling her to return home, found Sylvia and called for help. Sylvia was transported to a mental health facility, where she could recover. Marsha stayed by her friend's bedside throughout recovery and updated Sylvia on everyone's latest gossip. The two friends daydreamed about crossing the River Jordan together.

Shortly after Sylvia was discharged from the hospital, a close friend died from an overdose. The trauma Sylvia endured while living on Forty-Second Street and her involvement in the movement's early years had pushed her toward her breaking point. She decided it was time to take a break from community organizing and leave New York City.

Sylvia moved to Tarrytown, New York, a town located on the eastern bank of the Hudson River, north of Midtown Manhattan, where Sylvia had spent much of her life. While in Tarrytown, Sylvia lived with her partner in a suburban neighborhood and worked as a food service manager with Marriott Corporation. She eventually started her own catering company and began to expand her management skills. After her workday, Sylvia joined the growing local drag scene and eventually began helping plan community shows and events. She used what she learned from her time in New York City and brought the big city imagination to Tarrytown.

As Sylvia and her partner worked to create a stable life for themselves, it was important for Sylvia to remain linked to her friends in the Village. After all, they were still her family. She stayed connected to the community that had helped her grow while in New York City and traveled between cities to spend time with Marsha and others whenever she could.

By 1981 the discovery of an "unknown type of cancer" that was spreading throughout the city and country made headline news. When initial cases of AIDS were diagnosed among gay men, the public perceived the alarming epidemic to be the fault and issue of queer people. Government leaders ignored their role in encouraging public health as they also placed blame on the so-called immoral people.

HIV/AIDS is a virus contractible by any person regardless of gender or sexuality, yet discrimination and lack of basic needs left queer people exposed to the most severe of impacts. The late 1980s and early 1990s saw many, many community members dying from the disease. After countless deaths and little government response, AIDS Coalition to Unleash Power (ACT UP) challenged communities to

WHAT IS HIV/AIDS?

The human immunodeficiency virus, more commonly known as HIV, is a virus that attacks the body's immune system. When HIV is not treated, it may lead to acquired immunodeficiency syndrome, referred to as AIDS.

The first cases of HIV/AIDS in the United States were recorded in the early 1980s. At the time, little was known about the virus and it was thought to be a rare cancer. Social anxiety about the unknown virus that was quickly spreading led to accusations and blame. Because many gay men contracted the virus early, stigma evolved about HIV being a gay issue.

Political leaders encouraged stigma and homophobia by their own lack of action and condemnation of gay community members. The gay community was left to die, and many unfortunately did. Globally, thirty-nine million people have died since the HIV/AIDS epidemic began in the 1980s.

HIV/AIDS continues to have deep stigma, but much has also changed in how communities care for people who are living with HIV/AIDS. Research and community advocacy have helped to make the once-incurable virus treatable. As of 2022, three people have been reported to be cured from the virus.

break their silence and demand life-saving care. Those who lived and cared for their dying partners and friends were also transformed forever.

The public's discouraging response to the AIDS crisis mirrored its lack of concern about the ongoing physical violence faced by trans people.

Shortly after the Gay Pride parade in 1992, Marsha P. Johnson's body was found in the Hudson River. Marsha's death was declared a suicide early into the police investigation, but Marsha's friends demanded NYPD continue to search for what, or *who*, caused Marsha's death.

Before her death, Marsha and other street organizers vocalized the dangers they lived under, including corrupt cops and many forms of organized crime. Homeless communities are at high exposure to state violence, and therefore key witnesses to many incidents of violence. Simply because they are poor, homeless people are forced to be aware of unfair treatment and find ways to survive.

Marsha refused to be silent about the violence that trans people in the streets faced on a regular basis. As a mother to many homeless youth, Marsha was honest with her children about how power was abused by some lawmakers and law enforcement officers. Marsha's honesty and visibility made her a target. For these reasons, community members refused to accept NYPD's declaration of Marsha's cause of death as suicide. Marsha's death remains unresolved and representative of the ongoing violence faced by trans people, especially Black trans women.

When Sylvia received the telegram letting her know of Marsha's death, she thought about the River Jordan. They had promised each other to live long enough to cross the Jordan together.

Even though the idea of crossing the River Jordan was a simple Biblical metaphor, Marsha had crossed without Sylvia, who in her grief said, "Part of me went with her."

Sylvia was devastated by the loss of her closest friend and sister. At forty years old, Sylvia had been sober for nearly twenty years—since her suicide attempt in 1974—but she suddenly began struggling to maintain her sobriety and the stability she'd found in Tarrytown. Eventually, Sylvia lost her job and home in Tarrytown.

Sylvia moved back to New York City and set up camp on the piers near the familiar Forty-Second Street, a few blocks away from the Gay Community Center she had co-launched years before. Sylvia naturally assumed the role of mother to some of the young homeless campers around her, caring for them and sharing her wisdom with them.

When she was alone, she would stand out in front of her tent and watch the water of the Hudson River where Marsha was found.

As Sylvia grieved, she felt determined to help seek justice in honor of Marsha. She was frustrated by society's silence but refused to stop sounding the alarm. STAR members had always said the ongoing violence that trans and queer people were subject to would only end if society stopped rewarding violence.

Sylvia had spent more than half her life homeless and considered the likelihood of her escaping poverty slim. Yet being back in Manhattan, close to old and new friends, gave her hope and a purpose to move forward. Sylvia was ready to organize the community back into action.

In 1993, Sylvia was invited to move into Transy House, a community home inspired by STAR House decades prior. Here, Sylvia received the love and care she had dreamed of. She also met her life partner, Julia Murray, while living here, a relationship that would extend to the end of Sylvia's life.

"Everybody [at Transy House] calls me Ma—Ma Sylvia. We help everybody that we can and we get involved in everything that we can: Matthew Shepard, Diallo, Louima. We just go all over getting arrested."

Throughout the 1990s, many queer organizations had been established and gave the movement a different kind of infrastructure. The rise in resourced, nonprofit organizations was part of the movement's strategy to continue assimilating into mainstream society and power. By the late 1990s, queer organizations began securing resources that allowed for stronger, sustained community activation. The growing visibility of queer professionals and formal queer organizations fit into the narrative that community leaders strived for: acceptance. *We're just like you, just a little different, but not too different, we're just like you.* The problem with doing whatever it takes to gain acceptance, however, is that the stories that aren't easy to talk about get edited, skipped, or erased altogether.

Ongoing violence against trans people was kept out of national dialogue. One of the first queer-hate incidents of violence to garner national and international attention was the assault and murder of Matthew Shepard in 1998. Matthew was a gay college student at the University of Wyoming, and his death eventually led to hate-crime laws being put into place. Just as she did countless times before, Sylvia joined New York City–based protests to bring awareness not only to the deadly violence Matthew had experienced but also to the violence experienced by queer people everywhere.

The brutal killing of transgender woman Amanda Milan in 2000 fueled familiar cycles of devastation, anger, and urgency for local community, including Sylvia. Although there had been supportive momentum a few years prior, the lack of attention on Amanda's death confirmed that old patterns prevailed.

Sylvia relaunched STAR, with a slight shift in name: Street *Transgender* Action Revolutionaries. The group organized demonstrations around New York City and advocated for city leaders to create laws that specifically protected trans people. The Gay Rights Bill, which stemmed from the failed Intro 475, was the first type of nondiscrimination bill to have passed in 1986 but hadn't included STAR's concerns about discrimination against trans people.

In 2002, while STAR continued to advocate for legal protections, Sylvia became ill and was diagnosed with liver cancer. Her declining health had been a direct result of the years she spent coping with unstable housing and lack of community care. But Sylvia was unswayed in her determination to create change and use herself as a vessel for that change.

Always quick with strategy, Sylvia called on policymakers handling SONDA (Sexual Orientation Non-Discrimination Act) to come to her hospital room. From her bed, Sylvia explained the urgency of their campaign and the need to protect people like her. She made clear that SONDA was a necessary step in helping trans people keep themselves alive, even as she knew she wouldn't see its implementation.

Sylvia Lee Rivera died on February 19, 2002. Later that year, on December 17, SONDA passed in the State Senate and was signed into law.

WHAT IS SONDA?

SONDA stands for SEXUAL ORIENTATION NON-DISCRIMINATION ACT, a bill that was advocated for by New York City activists in the early 2000s. At the time, ongoing incidents of discrimination left many trans and queer people harmed, unemployed, or worse. Sylvia Rivera relaunched STAR, with the updated name Street Transgender Action Revolutionaries, after the murder of Amanda Milan in 2000. STAR and other community organizations demanded state lawmakers to finally protect trans and queer people under the law. SONDA protected individuals from discrimination based on sexual orientation at work, in school admissions, public services, and housing. Although the 2002 bill did not specifically include protections for gender identity, SONDA was interpreted to protect the rights of trans people if they were discriminated against based on their perceived sexual orientation.

SONDA was signed into New York law by Governor George Pataki in 2002. In 2019 New York Governor Andrew Cuomo signed the Gender Expression Non-Discrimination Act (GENDA), which added protections for gender identity.

Nondiscrimination policies are important and have continued to be advocated for by communities. There has yet to be a federal employee nondiscrimination act to pass Congress.

CHAPTER SIX

MOTHER OF A MOVEMENT

Sylvia's determination to live authentically was the life force that continued to persist even after her death in 2002. From the time she arrived at Forty-Second Street, Sylvia understood the high risk of embracing her truth in a culture that made it clear people like her were unwelcome. The lasting connections Sylvia created with other marginalized people throughout her life nourished her and others mutually, and this support system helped Sylvia reach for the stars. In a similar way, the loving kindness and fierce loyalty she offered others fueled the community's potential for creating change.

"Mothering" is about caring for children so they grow to thrive as adults beyond and because of the mother. Deeper than gender roles, mothering is both an evolutionary and revolutionary practice. For mamas like Sylvia and Marsha, mothering other kids was their way of caring for people who needed to be cared for, in the same ways older street queens cared for them as young teenagers. Regardless of gender, age, or looks, the intuitive bond between displaced trans, queer, and two-spirit people shows the interconnected bond of humanity. As mothers of endangered children, it was important that Sylvia and Marsha instill the skills and core values their kids needed to survive.

What Sylvia and STAR had been calling for, for more than three decades, was the right for all people to choose what to do with their bodies. They wanted to create a culture where people were encouraged to reach their potential, and where all communities are an important part of the story. Sylvia's life and advocacy were a testament to the power that each individual can bring into this world by embracing their truth.

Within a year of Sylvia's passing, her fierce spirit and visionary legacy helped catalyze the growing national movement for trans liberation. This time, her children were leading the way.

In August 2002, Dean Spade, a legal fellow and activist in New York City, opened a legal clinic to offer services and support to trans people who were struggling to navigate the legal system. The clinic was named the Sylvia Rivera Law Project (SRLP). SRLP organizers believed that people's right to self-determine their gender was undeniably linked to socioeconomic justice. Spade "sought to create an organization that addressed the severe poverty and over-incarceration" of low-income transgender communities of color, "understanding that meaningful political participation for people struggling against gender identity discrimination could only come in partnership with economic justice."

A year after opening, SRLP became a nonprofit organization, which provided a legally recognized status and the infrastructure to steadily build up its resources and impact. With a shared-leadership collective and range of community programs, SRLP has continued to advocate for gender justice through campaigns like #NoNewJailsNYC and the Trans Health Campaign to this day. The organization is run by staff and core collective members from the NYC community. Today, SRLP is housed within the Miss Major-Jay Toole Building for Social Justice on Forty-Second Street, which is home to a group of social justice organizations and freedom fighters.

MISS MAJOR GRIFFIN-GRACY (1940–PRESENT)

Miss Major was born in the southside of Chicago on October 25, 1940. As a young queer person, Miss Major found community in the Chicago ballroom scene. The balls were regular, underground spaces for queer kids to dress to the nines and dance against one another for trophies. Growing up during the 1940s and 1950s meant her gender expression was looked down upon.

Miss Major is a veteran of the Stonewall riots and survivor of Dannemora prison and Bellevue Hospital's "queen tank." As an advocate for transgender people, Miss Major has focused on supporting the survival of younger trans girls of color.

Miss Major's work as a movement leader is rooted in her commitment to change the world into a place where all people can thrive, regardless of gender. In the 1980s, Miss Major moved to New York City and joined in the community efforts to care for people living with HIV/AIDS. She also served as the director of San Francisco–based Transgender Gender-Variant & Intersex Justice Project (TGIJP), reentering prisons to connect with incarcerated community members.

Intent on doing what she can to support her people, Miss

> Major moved to Arkansas, where she could be closer to Southern trans communities who continue to be targeted based on gender identity. In Little Rock, Miss Major runs House of GG, a retreat center for trans and nonbinary leaders. Miss Major is a mother to many trans and queer younger people whom she has cared for over the years.

Also in 2002, the Transgender Law Center (TLC) was established as a project of the National Center for Lesbian Rights (NCLR) in California. Cofounded by Chris Daley and Dylan Vade, TLC was originally a California-based project focused on providing direct services to trans community members. In twenty years, TLC has grown into the nation's largest trans-specific, trans-led organization focused on self-determination for all people. As featured on their website, through "organizing and movement-building programs, TLC assists, informs, and empowers thousands of individual community members a year and builds towards a long-term, national, trans-led movement for liberation."

For marginalized people, community organizations and leadership are critical to keep a seat at the table of change-making. Because the gender binary and gender roles are so deeply ingrained in US culture, trans and gender-divergent people continue to experience cycles of erasure and violence that take new shapes over time.

In 2007, five years after the death of Sylvia, trans activists were caught on the losing side of another familiar compromise. Trans and queer organizations across the United States worked together to advocate for congressional support for the passing of a federal Employment Non-Discrimination Act (ENDA). The legislation aimed to prohibit discrimination based on sexual orientation but had been unsuccessfully introduced to Congress multiple times since 1974. Once the Democratic Party won a majority of seats in the 2006 midterm elections after more than a decade of Republican hold, community leaders believed their chance of passing ENDA had arrived. The 2007 ENDA bill introduced was the first version to include protection from gender discrimination, which had long been advocated for by Sylvia and other trans community members.

Fearing that including gender identity would create too much division, lawmakers proposed that the advocacy groups accept a draft of the bill that included protections based on sexual orientation but *not* gender identity. Removing protections for trans people threatened to leave behind the same group that experienced a similar betrayal in the 1970s with New York City's Intro 475. The Human Rights Campaign (HRC), a national queer advocacy organization who partnered with the bill's sponsor Barney Frank (D-MA) to pursue the legislation, was the only organization to sign a letter of support for the new bill.

The exclusion of gender protections activated trans leaders and resulted in an overnight coalition including sixty different organizations, United ENDA, which tried to stop the compromise and sacrifice of trans rights that was happening again. Although the gay-only version of ENDA passed Congress floors without including gender protections, it was never implemented as law. A federal protection for trans and queer people in employment, housing, and other areas of life has not been signed into law. As of 2022, just less than half of US states have full protection for trans and queer people.

Young people whose identities are shamed or criminalized are often forced into deciding between freedom and belonging. Historically, dominant cultures have tried to limit the free will and power of young people, often perceived as threats to matters of authority and control. Sylvia's refusal to fit into society's binary boxes lives on in the contemporary generation of trans and queer youth who embody her resilience and vision.

Today, there are many examples of trans and queer young people stepping into their potential and shaping change throughout the United States and the world. In the face of guardians and politicians who pressure trans and queer youth into conformity, community organizing and multimedia platforms have made it possible for each generation to start off with a little more of the care everybody deserves.

In the half century since the Stonewall riots, the queer, rebellious energy of the uprisings has persisted as young people take on active roles in transforming society toward liberation and freedom for all people, of all genders.

Black lesbian feminist bell hooks made it clear: The classroom remains the most radical space of possibility in academia. Whether it was the energy of student action or the reality that young people spent most of their time in school and on campus, trans, queer, and two-spirit (TQ2S)

youth began to create ways to end isolation and connect with others like them. By 1972, trans and queer students began openly gathering in student clubs like the Gay International Youth Society of George Washington High School in NYC. Across the country, early student clubs based on sexuality and gender were challenged by unsupportive administrations and pushback from parents and other members of the community. Young people who had been forced out of the school system organized community groups like STAR. School and community clubs rode the momentum of the post-Stonewall movement, giving students space to "assert their autonomy with vocal gusto."

Through the late 1970s and 1980s, most youth-focused support was through the lens of professionally managed social services.

Since the HIV/AIDS epidemic devastated trans and queer community health and well-being, support services were more concerned with saving TQ2S people rather than providing them with the tools for self-sufficiency. Throughout the 1990s, queer student clubs were established in schools nationwide, giving rise to Gay Straight Alliance clubs (GSAs), today commonly referred to as Genders & Sexualities Alliances. In 1998, twenty-three-year-old Carolyn Laub founded GSA Network, established as a national organization to support the growing network of student-led trans and queer groups. More than five thousand GSA clubs exist throughout the nation in high schools, middle schools, and elementary schools, and have connected with the organization in its two decades of building youth movements.

As the work of these and countless other justice organizations take root and grow, anxiety among conservative community leaders drives the array of anti-trans and anti-queer public campaigns. An investigative report published by TransLash Media in 2021 reveals the "highly organized political apparatus" they named the "Anti-Trans Hate Machine: A Plot Against Equality." Anchored by journalist and thought leader Imara Jones, the findings connect ongoing, nationwide attacks against trans people to a decades-long strategy and funding pool of three wealthy American families.

In 2015, Transgender Law Center and GSA Network partnered to create and launch a California-based youth program to fill the gaps in how gender-diverse youth leaders and storytellers were being resourced. The project focused on innovating different ways to support trans youth leaders who shared their stories as part of culture-shift activism. After a few years, the program expanded regionally and the National Trans Youth Council was launched. The TRUTH (TRans yoUTH) Project became the first national program led by and for transgender young people. The program aimed to uplift the leadership and vision of a cohort of trans and nonbinary youth leaders throughout the nation.

In 2018, the youth council drafted and published the TRUTH Nine-Point Platform. Building off the political platforms from groups like the Black Panther Party, Gay Liberation Front, Young Lords, STAR, and others, the trans youth manifesto called for an intersectional movement toward freedom for all peoples. Two years later, in 2020, the Transgender Law Center led a national, intergenerational coalition of trans leaders to draft and publish the *Trans Agenda for Liberation*. The *Trans Agenda* embodies the legacy of leaders like Sylvia Rivera and STAR members, as well as the leadership of trans youth today.

While trans communities continue to work together in order to survive, trans people have yet to experience full protection under the law. Since the 2015 Supreme Court ruling that legalized marriage between queer people, intense backlash has taken the form of discriminatory legislation brought to federal and state floors by conservative politicians. The amount of anti-trans legislation jumped from fewer than ten bills in 2020 to nearly two hundred anti-trans bills proposed in the spring of 2022.

Trans and queer people have long been forced to persist, even in moments of violence and suffering, even when not fully allowed to be themselves. This common exposure to the harmful side of societal systems that trans people, especially trans people of color, experience has reinforced the need for collective determination and action.

Sylvia Lee Rivera embodied this sense of freedom in every way she could. Through crisis and struggle, she challenged herself to march to the beat of her heart and resisted giving in to the easy ways of assimilation. Sylvia's learned experiences made clear to her, and those she passed on her wisdom to, the importance of practicing freedom every chance we have.

WHAT IS THE *TRANS AGENDA FOR LIBERATION*?

The TRANS AGENDA FOR LIBERATION (TA4L) is a community-led framework for trans liberation and organizing. The agenda includes five pillars that speak to important steps in building trans power. According to coalition leaders, the agenda was "put forward by a national coalition of majority Black, Indigenous, and migrant trans, nonbinary, and gender-nonconforming leaders" working with Transgender Law Center, the largest transgender advocacy organization in the United States.

TA4L breaks down the path toward liberation with the following pillars: Black trans femmes leading and living fiercely, beloved home, intergenerational connection and lifelong care, defining ourselves, right to thrive. The various pillars are interconnected and built on the work of trans people throughout generations, including Sylvia Rivera, Marsha P. Johnson, and STAR.

The leaders who drafted the agenda said, "We have challenged each other, supported each other's work, and dreamed about how we can realize a future where we are all free. Together, we birthed a framework to understand the forces harming our communities, and how we can unite to bring forward something new."

The idea of practicing freedom is made possible by the natural power and choices every person possesses simply by existing and being alive. Although society pressures individuals to keep themselves inside small boxes, individual power and choice can free everyone. Practicing freedom in everyday life requires people to bring freedom into their thoughts, actions, and beliefs.

A free mind is one that releases the expectations society places on young people's shoulders. This requires that young people learn how to listen to themselves and to find the space and community for their truth to be heard. Sylvia believed each person, each star, deserved the space to shine.

Sylvia lived her life constantly giving her body the permission to flow as it wished. Having witnessed many women throughout her life be robbed of their body's agency, Sylvia moved heart-strong toward ending violence and affirming everybody's right to *be*. She dreamed of a future free from violence and knew she had to bring that future into the present. Her exposure to police brutality and protests while living on the street pushed her to learn the power of her body and the space she could take up. By refusing to blend in and silence herself, Sylvia showed her community how to embody freedom every day.

Sylvia's prayer for a free spirit was rooted in her understanding that life itself is the gift. Humans, of any gender experience, are good as we are. This was the fiery life force within her fierce and loving spirit that New York City, and the world, knew Sylvia to be.

To honor life (Sylvia's life and our own), we must learn from the wisdom Sylvia and STAR always pointed us toward. Stonewall was never about erasing who we are for acceptance. In Sylvia's words, the point was always simple: to live.

"It's fun just being Sylvia."

DID YOU KNOW?

★ Sylvia Rivera is considered one of the pivotal figures who ensured the "T" in LGBTQ.

biography.com/activist/sylvia-rivera

★ The Sylvia Rivera Law Project continues her legacy, working to guarantee "all people are free to self-determine their gender identity and expression, regardless of income or race, and without facing harassment, discrimination, or violence."

srlp.org/about/

★ The intersection of Christopher and Hudson Streets in Greenwich Village, two blocks from the Stonewall Inn, was renamed "Sylvia Rivera Way" in 2005.

nypl.org/blog/2021/01/29/sylvia-rivera

★ In 2015, a portrait of Rivera was added to the National Portrait Gallery in Washington, DC, making her the first transgender activist to be included in the gallery.

npg.si.edu/blog/welcome-collection-sylvia-rivera

advocate.com/transgender/2015/10/27/sylvia-rivera-gets
-place-national-portrait-gallery

★ In 2019, New York City announced plans to unveil a monument to Rivera and Johnson. It will be the city's—and according to New York City, the world's—first monument dedicated to transgender individuals. The statue was supposed to go up in 2021, but the COVID-19 pandemic has delayed the monuments.

womenshistory.org/education-resources/biographies/sylvia
-riveragothamist.com/arts-entertainment/marsha-p-johnson
-statue-bust-christopher-park

★ Rivera delivered her fiery "Y'all Better Quiet Down" speech in New York City at the Christopher Street Liberation Day Rally in Washington Square Park in 1973 amid boos from the crowd.

biography.com/activist/sylvia-rivera

★ In 1994, Rivera was honored at the twenty-fifth anniversary celebration of the Stonewall Inn riots.

britannica.com/biography/Sylvia-Rivera

★ She refused to label her identity, referring herself sometimes as a gay man, a gay girl, or a drag queen. Mostly she identified herself simply as Sylvia.

transadvocate.com/in-revolution-the-trans-terms-sylvia-rivera-used_n_13623.htm

★ The MCC New York's queer youth shelter is named "Sylvia's Place" in her honor.

sylviariverasplace.com/about

★ An off-Broadway musical *Sylvia So Far*, based on her life, ran between 2007 and 2008.

wanderwomenproject.com/women/sylvia-rivera/

★ Sylvia was inducted into the Legacy Walk in Chicago, Illinois.

legacyprojectchicago.org/person/sylvia-rivera

★ The World Health Organization removed transsexuality from its list of mental illnesses only in June 2018.

aldianews.com/en/culture/heritage-and-history/sylvia-riveras-struggle

STUDENT GLOSSARY & RESOURCES

LATINX/LATINE: refers to people of Latin American origin or descent; *Latinx* has been primarily been used by English speakers, whereas LGBTQ+ Spanish speakers have adopted the use of *Latine*.

TRANSGENDER: people who experience gender differently than what was assigned to them at birth.

QUEER: describes non-normative gender identities, meaning someone who is not cisgender (see below) and relationships between people who are not heterosexual (see below).

CISGENDER: people whose gender identity corresponds with the gender they were assigned at birth.

HETEROSEXUAL: a person or relationship characterized by romantic attraction to people of the opposite sex, specifically between a cisgender man and cisgender woman.

TWO-SPIRIT (2S): a term generally describing Indigenous experiences with queer relationships and genders; two-spirit people may also identify with terms in their people's language.

TQ2S: an acronym (or abbreviation of the first letter of the words) that can describe the general trans, queer, and two-spirit communities/population; other choices that have been used include LGBT, GLBT, LGBTQ+, QT.

POVERTY: having a severe lack of basic needs security (stable housing, food, resources).

JUSTICE: determining rights according to law or equity; when relating to social justice, it focuses on balancing what is right and fair for people regardless of their socioeconomic background.

OPPRESSION: the set of behaviors and obstacles that are meant to maintain a divide between "us" and "them."

If you or someone you know would like to learn more about the LGBTQ+ community and their resources, visit the following pages:

GSA NETWORK: Genders & Sexualities Alliances (GSAs) are trans, queer, and allied youth building communities. They are student-run organizations that unite LGBTQ+ and allied youth to organize around issues impacting them in their schools and communities. If you want to start a GSA club at your school, visit GSA Network at **GSANetwork.org**.

TRANS LIFELINE: Run by and for trans people, Trans Lifeline is a hotline and nonprofit organization that offers direct emotional and financial support to trans people in crisis. **TransLifeline.org**

THE TREVOR PROJECT: The Trevor Project is a suicide-prevention and mental-health organization for LGBTQ+ (lesbian, gay, bisexual, transgender, queer, and questioning) young people where they can reach out to a counselor if they're struggling, find answers and information, and get the tools they need to help someone else. **TrevorProject.org**

GENDER JUSTICE LEADERSHIP PROGRAMS (GJLP) AND NATIONAL TRANS YOUTH COUNCIL (TRUTH): GJLP and TRUTH are youth-led programs for trans and gender-nonconforming young people to build public understanding, empathy, and a movement for liberation through storytelling and media organizing. **OurTransTruth.org**

AN INVITATION TO READERS

In researching and sharing Sylvia's story, I wanted to honor and expand what we know of our movement's history as trans, queer, and two-spirit people. What's remembered lives. Legendary trans journalist Monica Roberts and her work of writing about the lives of trans people was an example of this. Storytelling is a way that people have kept the past and all its wisdom alive . . . which is probably why our parents and grandparents take their time retelling their extra-long, detailed stories of yesterday. Listen to those tales. And one day, when the moment feels right, share your own story.

There are many ways to move through this book. So take what is useful at the time you're reading this, then return again to dig in with new questions. I wrote this to be a solid starting place for you to lean on when reaching back to the past. Whether you're working on a biography report or trying to learn more about your peoples' movement, this is an invitation:

> Remember and learn your history.
> Be sure you live fully, every day.
> Create your piece of the future!
> ... No pressure. "It's fun!" Sylvia told me.

Learn Your History

How did you get here?

As humans, we can remember our lineage and where we come from! This is a cool evolution of our brains. Sharing stories through words, song, and art has also helped groups of people survive.

So make sure to gather up important learnings from those before us and bring them with you into the present day and tomorrow.

Live Fully, Every Day

What do you think about this?

When I was in school, I tried to learn all the facts and remember them for tests—this is what we were taught learning was about. But that's not how my brain works best, or any of ours, actually. We're not machines that can take in and give out data with no feeling. Whatever we touch, we change, and it changes us. So make sure to add your magic to this world, too.

Create and Share the Future!

Where are we going?

My mom would remind me, often, that my sisters were the only people connected with me forever. I'm happy to be learning that she was mostly right—our siblings can be incredible cheerleaders through growing pains. But we can also be forever connected with people we chose. Either way, find your part in this beloved global community—everyone has one.

A NOTE FROM J. GIA LOVING

Patrick Cordova was born October of 1996. That's me—Gia. I've changed a lot in only twenty-five years, including things like my name. Choosing my own name was one of the first ways I chose to be myself, and the many times I've changed my name since the first are also moments of me trusting myself.

Growing up, people around me spent a lot of time pointing out how other I was, which usually felt like them explaining to me why I was wrong. I tried to figure out what the right way to be was for many years. I studied the way people talked and walked and told stories. The more I worked to perform what I thought others wanted of me, the more I only felt disconnected from myself. I felt like a piñata, layers and layers slowly glued on.

I often wondered while daydreaming in class . . . *Why aren't young people ever taught that they are whole, creative, wonderful beings, just as they are?*

Instead, the American public education system trains students to become workers. Parts of a bigger, money-making machine. Apparently, the one way to live a good

American life is to spend it trying to own the entire machine. If working can earn you money, and money can buy you power, perhaps power can force you to be happy?

For many trans, queer, and two-spirit young people growing up around the world, we must often choose between living as our whole selves and feeling safe. After years of silently and quickly making these mental decisions, sometimes nanosecond decisions, I started to forget the parts of me I'd pushed down. This is their goal, I guessed—to have me forget the queer pieces of me with roots so deep, deep, deep inside of me. And in order to continue to be accepted and survive, I continued on burying parts of me. All in the dreams of one day being whole.

It took me a long time to meet people who told me straight-up: Some things you were told and taught (especially by bullies and tired parents) are not the whole story.

Uhh . . . so what is the whole story? I would ask. Before they could respond, I'd add: *Is who I am wrong? Is what feels so true to me wrong?*

Yet, no matter how many people I asked these questions to, no one could convince the small voice inside—young Giapatrick who survived too many years being told she was wrong, simply and mainly, because of who she was.

I needed another story, one I wasn't hearing yet but

have always felt. Then I finally slowed my mind enough to hear what was there all along.

By listening to and trusting myself, I began to hear so much more of my story.

The cool thing about our lives being our own stories to write and share with the universe is that every moment is part of that journey. Every deep breath. Every little growth. Every annoying, kinda-funny hiccup. Every younique talent. And with this being your story, only you get to write yourself in!

When we experience or witness transphobia and queerphobia, we may catch ourselves really wondering if it's possible to erase who we are. Looking back on even the last fifty years of TQ2S young peoples' lives, let alone human history, listen to what Miss Major once said: "We're still effin here."

By the way, if no one has told you yet, my beloved reader, you are a whole and wonderful being just as you are.

A NOTE FROM HISPANIC STAR

When Hispanic Star decided to join Macmillan and Roaring Brook Press in creating this chapter book biography series, our intention was to share stories of incredible Hispanic leaders with young readers, inspiring them through the acts of those Stars. For centuries, the Hispanic community has made significant contributions to different spaces of our collective culture—whether it's sports, entertainment, art, politics, or business—and we wanted to showcase some of the role models who made this possible. We especially wanted to inspire Latinx children to rise up and take the mantle of Hispanic unity and pride.

With Hispanic Star, we also wanted to shine a light on the common language that unifies a large portion of the Latinx community. *Hispanic* means "Spanish speaking" and frequently refers to people whose origins are from a country where Spanish is the primary spoken language. The term *Latinx*, in all its ever-changing deviations, refers to people of all gender identities from all countries in Latin America and their descendants, many of them already born in the United States.

This groundbreaking book series can be found both in English and Spanish as a tribute to the Hispanic community in our country.

We encourage all of our readers to get to know these heroes and the positive impact they continue to have, inviting future generations to learn more about the different journeys of our unique and charming Hispanic Stars!

THE HISPANIC STAR SERIES

Read about the most groundbreaking, iconic Hispanic heroes who have shaped our culture and the world in this gripping biography series for young readers.

IF YOU CAN SEE IT, YOU CAN BE IT.